Memories of Madness

A Collection of Stories from Inside a Mental Hospital

Bo Bowen

Memories of Madness

Memories of Madness

A Collection of Stories from Inside a Mental Hospital

Mississippi State Hospital
Whitfield, MS
1969-1970 & 1972-1978

Bo Bowen

Doctor's Dreams Publishing
Edited by Anita Bryan

Cover Photo Credit: Donald Golden Photography, "Chariot," 2021, via https://donaldgoldenphotography.shootproof.com/gallery/bestimages.
Back Cover Photo Credit: Barry Plunkett

Data: Bowen, Bo. Memories of Madness. A Collection of Stories from Inside a Mississippi Mental Hospital. 1969–1970 & 1972–1978: A Memoir / by Bo Bowen. Includes bibliographical references. Subjects: LCSH: Mississippi State Hospital—History. | Mental health services—Mississippi. | Insane Asylum — Mississippi. Mentally Ill—Mississippi. Mental hospitals—Mississippi—History. | Mental health workers—Mississippi—Biography. | Social work—Mississippi—Biography. | Whitfield—Mississippi. Attendants—Mental health services—Mississippi. Classification: LCC RC445.M7 BIO003000

DDC 362.21—dc23 ISBN: 978-1-942181-61-3

Published by Doctor's Dreams Publishing, Biloxi, Mississippi. Printed in the United States of America.

Memories of Madness is a memoir that reflects on the author's recollections of working in a mental hospital. All documents, photos, and art are from the author's personal collection. Used by permission, all rights reserved.

This book includes information that mentions and/or references Mississippi State Hospital; however, neither Mississippi State Hospital nor the Mississippi Department of Mental Health, nor its employees were actively involved in the development of this book. Further, views expressed and/or information contained within this book do not represent the opinions of Mississippi State Hospital or the Mississippi Department of Mental Health.

DEDICATION

To my family and friends who encouraged me to record these memories.
Thank you for believing these stories were worth preserving. Your support gave me the courage to revisit years that were meaningful, difficult, and unforgettable.

This dedication is also to Mary Helen Bowen, who had to listen to these stories for the last forty years.

PREFACE

This memoir began as a collection of memories I carried for decades—moments from the patient wards, from working with physicians, nurses, attendants, and social workers, and from the faces of people whose lives intersected with mine during my years at Mississippi State Hospital. And yes, there was some madness we all endured. I never set out to write a history of the institution nor to judge the people who worked within its walls. What I offer instead is a personal account of what I saw, what I learned, and how those years shaped me. The hospital I entered in 1969 was a world unto itself. It was a place where the old ways of institutional care were still firmly in place, even as new ideas about mental health were beginning to take hold. When I returned in 1972 as a social worker, I saw the hospital from a different angle—not just the daily routines of the wards but the emotional and bureaucratic weight carried by the staff. Names and identifying details of patients have been changed to protect privacy, but the experiences remain true to the time, the place, and the people who lived them.

Introduction

My given name is Ernest Lake Bowen, III. I have always signed all my legal documents and applications that way. However, I have never liked that name, much less its derivatives. Even in high school, I ignored students who called me Ernie, Ernestine, or Ernesto. My nickname prior to my birth was "Bunny," as in "rabbit." I have been called this name my entire life by family, friends, my parents' friends, neighbors, and anyone else who loved me. Maybe I was named for the famous big band jazz trumpeter, Bunny Berigan, or maybe my sister did not want a baby brother but a baby bunny rabbit. Whatever! Just don't call me Ernest!

I graduated from Tupelo High School in 1966 and enrolled at Mississippi State University, majoring in Business and Marketing. Why, I do not know, other than my dad said that is what I should do. I changed my major many times because I could not settle on what I wanted to do with my life. I skipped classes and faced academic probation several times. Except for being a member of The Famous Maroon Band or singing with the Travelers, a folk group I co-formed with a friend in high school, I was miserable! I was proud to pledge KA (as one of the oldest pledges), but I did not make my grades and had to leave the KA Order. There were added emotional issues that I was trying to tackle, and because I was on academic probation, I had to sit out a semester before I could re-enroll.

While on academic probation in 1969, I realized I should have chosen a major that would have been more interesting, thus motivating me to study. At that time, however, I didn't have any interests outside of music. Then, during my semester off, an opportunity presented itself for me to work as an attendant during the summer at the Mississippi State Hospital at Whitfield, Mississippi. At that time, the hospital hired college students for the summer. I jumped on it.

When I first walked onto the grounds in 1969, I was young, unsure, and unprepared for what I was about to encounter. I didn't know then that the hospital would become one of the defining places of my life. The wards were crowded, the routines strict, and the work demanding in ways I couldn't have imagined. As an attendant, I learned quickly the job required more than physical strength. It required patience, compassion, and a willingness to see humanity in people the world had largely forgotten. Some days were chaotic, some heartbreaking, and some unexpectedly full of humor.

I worked as an attendant (now classified as Mental Health Technician) in the Maximum-Security Unit for the Criminally Insane—an experience I will never forget. This job was a good fit for me. The building was called Cottage S (for security), and my job was guarding patients.

Later, meeting Evelyn Ayers, the hospital's Director of Nursing, I told her of my desire to continue working as a full-time employee in Male Receiving after my summer job ended. To the disappointment of my parents, I was not ready to return to college. Ms. Ayres agreed to hire me as a full-time employee with a salary of $225 a month. Subsequently, I was "cut off" financially from my parents. I considered this period a time of reckoning or an escape from other responsibilities in life. Which one was it?

Over the next year, I met many of the social workers who worked in the Male Receiving building and learned about their jobs and responsibilities with patients and physicians. I befriended Kathryn Guice, Director of Social Services, who took an interest in me. She offered me a position as a social worker if I returned to college to get a degree. I knew from my experience working as an attendant and from my association with social workers that I did, indeed, want to re-enroll at Mississippi State and earn a degree. I would become a social worker!

That I did with my parents' blessings. However, their deal was that I had to cut my long hair and shave off my beard. It was an adjustment to buckle down and study, but I made myself do it and even made the dean's list a couple of times. I continued to receive encouragement in the form of letters from Mary Belle McDonald, one of the social workers at Whitfield. She inspired me to study and get my degree. She also reminded me that Ms. Guice would hire me upon my graduation.

Graduating in 1972 with a degree in educational psychology and a minor in history, I returned to Mississippi State Hospital and was hired as a social worker. I saw the paperwork behind every patient's story, the families who struggled to understand, and the staff who tried to balance limited resources with genuine care. I witnessed the slow shift in mental-health treatment during the 1970s—a time when old systems were breaking down faster than new ones could replace them.

This memoir is not an attempt to speak for everyone who lived or worked at Mississippi State Hospital. It is simply my account—the stories I carried, the lessons I learned, and the people who stayed with me long after I left the grounds for the last time. Over the years, I met and talked with thousands of patients. I heard their stories and their songs. I saw their art and observed their life on the Whitfield campus. But there was also a dark side. Sometimes I dealt with their anger and disappointment or with the sadness and depression of those patients who had no family except for their family at Whitfield. In such cases, I would help them by providing them with resources to make their lives easier at the hospital.

There was always an element of danger lurking in the background, but sometimes there was something to laugh about. I was to learn that humor would be my saving grace when dealing with trouble. From my experience working with patients, psychiatrists, psychologists, nurses, social workers, attendants, and administrators, I was able to understand the history and the culture of Mississippi State Hospital. I could describe it from both a patient's historical account and my own personal involvement and experiences. In short, working with the staff, health care professionals, and patients was very gratifying and full of adventure. I also created my own adventures playing pranks on our office staff, writing funny memos, and just being silly and outrageous.

This book presents those stories and observations (based on my memory) of the time I worked at Whitfield. It is these experiences and memories that I want to share with those who may be curious about the history and culture of the Mississippi State Hospital and what it was like working with the mentally ill. I am sure other employees could correct or question my interpretations of the events I witnessed, but to the best of my knowledge, this is how life was at Whitfield over fifty-five years ago. Letters, memos, photos, and patient art are my personal property. I may have been a packrat, but I am glad now that I kept everything to share a part of my life's work at Whitfield through this book.

First, however, I want to share information about the Mississippi State Lunatic Asylum and the Mississippi State Hospital at Whitfield. When I was first hired, I did not know the full history of the hospital nor that of the old Asylum in Jackson, Mississippi.

The Mississippi State Lunatic Asylum

In January 1846, Governor A. G. Brown (1844-1848) proposed an asylum for Mississippi's insane. In February of that year, legislation was brought forth to build a State Lunatic Asylum in the capital city of Jackson, but the legislation was not passed into law. In 1848, Governor Brown again made his plea to the Mississippi Legislature, stating, "It is a reproach to any Christian people that lunatics and insane persons should go at large, unprotected by the care of their fellows, constantly exposed to danger themselves, and putting in imminent peril the lives and property of others."[1] That year, he signed an act appropriating $10,000, but that funding was insufficient. The Asylum was to be located on a tract of land in Jackson that is currently the location of the University of Mississippi Medical Center.

Ms. Dorothea L. Dix, nationally known as the "Angel of Mercy" for her work as a social reformer, was devoted to the welfare of the mentally ill. For forty years, she lobbied states to establish humane asylums for the mentally ill by documenting the conditions and treatment of patients. She had estimated from Mississippi's 1840 Census that there could be 450 to 500 insane people in Mississippi by 1850. Dix made a presentation to the Mississippi Legislature in 1850 about the state's insane:

It will be seen that Mississippi is one of the few states in which no provision has yet been supplied for the recovery of the demented and the maniac. But there are many who languish in inappropriate habitations, in wretched poverty-stricken dwellings, in ill-directed poorhouses, in exposed pens, or in dreary, unlighted, and unventilated cells, chargeable only with incapacity for self-care, and irresponsible by reason of sickness, physical infirmity, and the breaking down of the fortress of reason.[2]

She was able to secure an additional appropriation of $50,000 from the legislature for the construction of the Asylum.

It took seven long years, but after several requests for additional appropriations from the legislature, after construction problems, and after a yellow fever epidemic, the Mississippi State Lunatic Asylum finally opened its doors on January 8, 1855. It was four stories high with two wings. The center was sixty-four feet across and one hundred feet deep, including a portico across the front. Until 1894, the Asylum relied on coal oil lamps and candles for lighting. At that time, it could provide services for only 150 patients. By 1856, in the pre-Civil War era, a few slaves and free persons of color were admitted.

Even when it opened in 1855, funding was lacking for the Asylum because the care of the insane was not a priority of the state legislature. Consequently, the state continued to struggle to provide the funding needed. Ms. Dix returned to Mississippi in 1858 and was able to persuade the legislature to appropriate additional funding for the expansion of the institution, as the Asylum was already overcrowded.

Courtesy of the Asylum Projects, Image property of Soldat.https:///www.asylumprojects.org/index.php/File:Jackson_State_Hospital.jpg.

The State Lunatic Asylum endured the "Siege of Jackson" during the Civil War. Federal troops invaded Jackson in July 1863, and a corps encamped around the grounds of the Asylum.

The cupola (dome) of the main building was occupied as a signal station. The Confederates were under the impression that the Federals had removed the patients and began firing on the building. Fortunately, the mistake was found in time to prevent any personal damage to the patients or the institution.[3]

General William T. Sherman left the Asylum intact but slaughtered livestock and ransacked the pantries and gardens. Seven of the Asylum's ten employees left their jobs and joined the Union Army. The Asylum was without food or clothing for the patients, and there was no funding available from the state. Dr. Robert Kells, the first superintendent of the Asylum, was able to acquire bales of cotton that he traded with the Federal soldiers in Vicksburg for food and clothing for the inmates. Only through Kells' persistence and the approval of Civil War Governor Charles Clark was he successful in making this exchange.

At the end of the Civil War, federal troops were brought into Jackson, and military commanders administered the government of Mississippi. Governor Clark was arrested in 1865 and sent to prison with Jefferson Davis, President of the Confederacy. They were imprisoned at Fort Pulaski in Savanna, Georgia, as prisoners of war.

***

Reconstruction in the South began at the end of the Civil War in 1865 and remained until 1877, when federal troops were withdrawn from the states. Allan Branstiter, USM graduate of the Dale Center for the Study of War and Society, authored a 2016 blog about Reconstruction in the Mississippi State Insane Asylum in which he noted that the Asylum was not necessarily cut off from activities during Reconstruction. Branstiter's article in *News Magazine,* published by the American Historical Association, points out "Jackson's elite frequently visited the institution, participated in its "lunatic balls," and supported it financially when the government could not."[4]

In 1870, Dr. William Compton was appointed superintendent and served until 1878. He was able to obtain support from the governor and the legislature to improve housing for the "lunatics of color" to equal that provided for the Whites. He acknowledged, with (Governor) "Alcorn's support, the need for segregation by both race and sex."[5] Black patients resided in the same building with white patients but lived in separate wards. Segregation of the races at the Asylum and at Mississippi State Hospital in Whitfield remained in place until the passage of the Civil Rights Act of 1964. This act outlawed discrimination based on race, color, religion, sex, and national origin. Integration of the Whitfield campus began in 1965 and went without incident.

Dr. C. D. Mitchell was the superintendent of the Asylum from 1918 to 1926 and from 1930-1940. He pleaded with the legislature to enlarge the hospital, but he recommended to the legislature that no improvements be made at that time. "Due to overcrowding and the infectious nature of tuberculosis, patients at the Jackson asylum with this disease were housed in tents on the front lawn of the asylum."[6] There had also been a yellow fever epidemic, and Dr. Mitchell suggested a second institution be built outside the Jackson area to absorb the crowded conditions at the Asylum.

In 1882, the legislature appropriated funding for the construction of a hospital on land donated by citizens of Meridian, Mississippi. The land was originally established under the Treaty of Dancing Rabbit Creek in 1830 during the period of Indian removal. The East Mississippi Insane Asylum opened in January 1885. Even though the East Mississippi Asylum was only ninety miles from Jackson, it did not relieve the overcrowding in the Jackson hospital.

In 1892, a fire broke out in Jackson's Asylum, destroying two-thirds of the institution's major building. It claimed one patient's life. Spurred by this devastating fire, the state legislature appropriated funds in 1894 to install electric light fixtures throughout the institution.

The hospital had a light plant, an ice factory, sewing rooms, a bakery, a butcher shop, an orchard, a dairy, and a florist. It was fully equipped with an operating room, an X-ray room, and a laboratory. Because the Occupational Therapy Department was designed to help patients return to a "normal mental condition by means of occupation…it was self-supporting. Here, all mattresses, mops, brooms, and rugs are made."[7]

***

The legislature appropriated funding for the construction of a new hospital for the insane in the rural Howell community in Rankin County. The hospital would be located fifteen miles southeast of Jackson on state-owned land that was formerly the Rankin County State Farm. The Mississippi State Insane Hospital was renamed the Mississippi State Hospital in 1926, and the location of the hospital was named Whitfield in honor of Governor Henry L. Whitfield, who was in office when the legislature first voted to build the hospital. While the hospital's name officially changed to the Mississippi State Hospital, some continued to identify it as the "Asylum" as long as it remained at that location in Jackson.

Ground was broken on February 10, 1928, for the new hospital, but it would be nine more years before patients would be transferred from the Asylum to the new Mississippi State Hospital at Whitfield. The initial grading of the hospital "was done with labor from the convict farm located near the site. The farm was a branch of the notorious Parchman State Penitentiary. With supervision by E. Q. White, caretaker of the farm, the convicts accomplished all the grading for roads and terracing around buildings and quite a bit of excavation for the system of tunnels which connect the buildings."[8] Reinforced concrete tunnels connected all buildings on the campus to permit steam, water, sewerage pipes, and electricity to function. In later years, however, patients would sometimes access these tunnels to sleep, escape, or enter other buildings.

The Mississippi State Hospital at Whitfield was completed at a cost of $5,000,000, built on a 3,333-acre tract comprised of seventy-five red brick cottages with white columns that could accommodate 3,500 patients. A patient I knew at Whitfield called the cottages “red brick cemeteries.” The hospital opened its doors on March 4, 1935, with the transfer of more than 2,500 patients from the Asylum.

Whitfield would be the name commonly used for the hospital. Like the old state insane hospital, Whitfield would have many of the same features to become self-sufficient and self-sustaining. The hospital was designed to have a power plant, a laundry, a bakery, and repair shops. Half of the acreage would be devoted to farming, orchards, pastures, truck farms, and dairy.

The hospital was divided into two services, “one for the white patients and one for the colored patients.” The western side of the campus was for the Black patients and the eastern side for Whites. The Mississippi Code of 1930, section 4542, Laws Pertaining to Mental Hospitals, required that the white and colored races be kept separate in the hospital.[9]

Mississippi State Hospital, Whitfield – Summer of 1969

On May 30, 1969, I signed the Subversive Activities statement and checked that I would report to work on June 2, 1969, for a monthly salary of $225. I had no idea what subversive activities could take place at Whitfield, but I was signing that I would not overthrow the government. I was fingerprinted at the

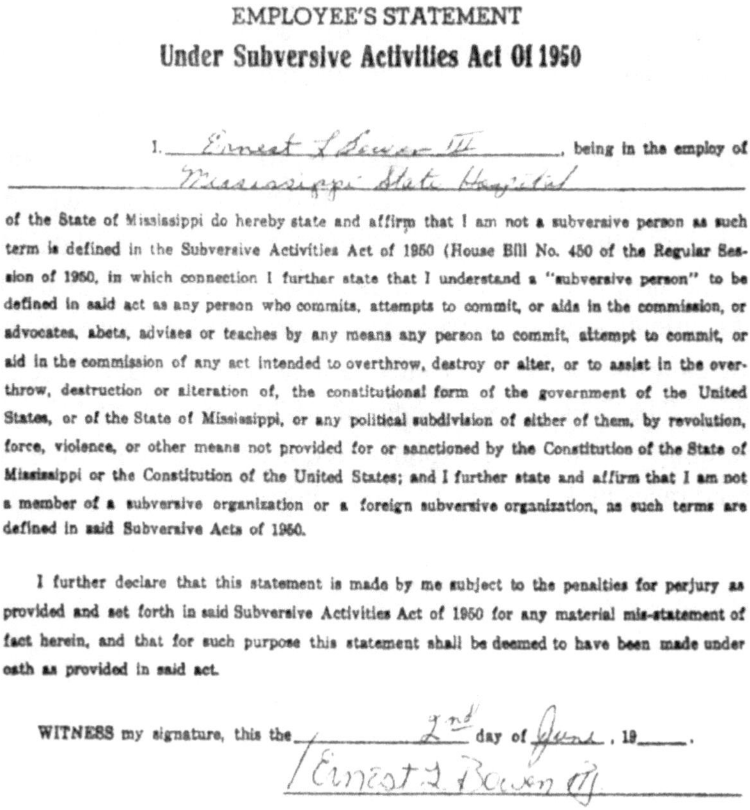

EMPLOYEE'S STATEMENT

Under Subversive Activities Act Of 1950

I, Ernest L Bowen III, being in the employ of Mississippi State Hospital of the State of Mississippi do hereby state and affirm that I am not a subversive person as such term is defined in the Subversive Activities Act of 1950 (House Bill No. 450 of the Regular Session of 1950, in which connection I further state that I understand a "subversive person" to be defined in said act as any person who commits, attempts to commit, or aids in the commission, or advocates, abets, advises or teaches by any means any person to commit, attempt to commit, or aid in the commission of any act intended to overthrow, destroy or alter, or to assist in the overthrow, destruction or alteration of, the constitutional form of the government of the United States, or of the State of Mississippi, or any political subdivision of either of them, by revolution, force, violence, or other means not provided for or sanctioned by the Constitution of the State of Mississippi or the Constitution of the United States; and I further state and affirm that I am not a member of a subversive organization or a foreign subversive organization, as such terms are defined in said Subversive Acts of 1950.

I further declare that this statement is made by me subject to the penalties for perjury as provided and set forth in said Subversive Activities Act of 1950 for any material mis-statement of fact herein, and that for such purpose this statement shall be deemed to have been made under oath as provided in said act.

WITNESS my signature, this the 2nd day of June, 19____.

Ernest L. Bowen III

Subversive Activities Statement, Property of Bo Bowen

Whitfield post office in the administration building, and was sent to the general hospital for a physical, which I passed as I was "acceptable." No Blood Wasserman test was done--probably because I convinced the doctors and nurses that I had a fear of needles--which I still do to this day.

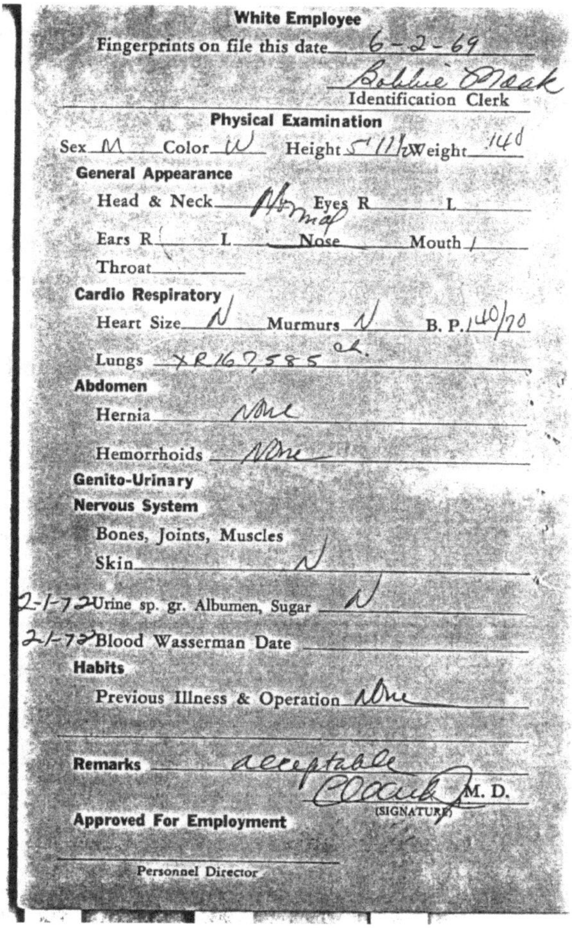

White Employee

Fingerprints on file this date 6-2-69

Bobbie Meak
Identification Clerk

Physical Examination

Sex M Color W Height 5'11½ Weight 140

General Appearance

Head & Neck Normal Eyes R L

Ears R L Nose Mouth

Throat

Cardio Respiratory

Heart Size N Murmurs N B. P. 140/70

Lungs XR 167,585 ok.

Abdomen

Hernia None

Hemorrhoids None

Genito-Urinary

Nervous System

Bones, Joints, Muscles

Skin N

2-1-72 Urine sp. gr. Albumen, Sugar N

2-1-72 Blood Wasserman Date

Habits

Previous Illness & Operation None

Remarks acceptable

M. D.
(SIGNATURE)

Approved For Employment

Personnel Director

Physical Examination Form. Property of Bo Bowen

I was assigned a room in the Male Employees' Dormitory. I cannot remember my roommate's name, but he was a short, balding man who was an attendant on one of the back-service buildings. Most male and female attendants wore white uniforms. Summer student employees could wear jeans and a shirt. The dormitory was a large building on the east side of the campus with a front porch with chairs. There was a day room with chairs and a TV. Showers and toilets were down the hall from our room. The dormitory was home to these men, and typically, their rooms were not tastefully decorated. Salaries were low, and the men, in most cases, had no other affordable place to live. The hospital served three meals a day, and all employees could buy a cheap meal ticket. I believe on the weekends, we had to make do with the food we might have in our room or go into Jackson to eat. I don't remember any of the men owning a car. For transportation, hospital employees and patients with town privileges would use the Whitfield bus to Jackson, which made round-trip trips between the hospital and the Greyhound Bus Station. The bus would run several times a day and in the evening. My friends who came with me from Mississippi State, a few medical students, and I all lived in the dormitory, and we always left the hospital at night to find things to do in Jackson. There was nothing to do on the campus at night other than watch TV. I owned a 1954 Ford Mainline I named "Old Blue," and it could always be found at Shakey's Pizza Parlor in Fondren, where the beer and pizzas were cheap. There was a Dixie Land duo with red-striped shirts who played there most nights, and I often got up and played the washtub bass.

Old Blue. Photo by Bo Bowen.

My car was well known late at night to the security officers at the hospital's front gate who would just wave us in, knowing where we had been all night.

***

There was a tall, lanky man who worked at the hospital dairy and lived in the dormitory. He often could be found hiding behind the bushes in front of the dormitory. My roommate told me the dairy worker was shell-shocked from WWII, and loud noises and other stimuli would upset him so much that he would crouch down to try to hide behind the bushes. I believe he had a room to himself. There were other characters living in the dorm, and many times we felt as if we were living in a back service cottage with the patients.

Further down the street from the Male-Employee Dormitory was the Female-Employee Dormitory, set up like the male dormitory. The living arrangements for married employees were in a building closer to the back service buildings. Dr. William Parker remembered that the former TB hospital for Black people had patients on the first floor and employees living on the second floor.

Dr. William (Bill) Parker, long-time physician at Whitfield, wrote a document titled "Believe It or Not!!!!! Isolated Remembrances (Hopefully Accurate) of the Early 70s to Early 80s at Mississippi State Hospital." I have referenced several of his observations that relate to my stories. Dr. Parker interned at MSH from 1970 to 1971 and was employed from 1971 to 1999.[10]

Don't Call Me Ernest!

After my college years when I started working, I was in a dilemma about what name to go by. I was employed at Mississippi State Hospital as an attendant from 1969 through 1970 and again from 1972 to 1978 as a social worker. When I first started during the summer of 1969, I was addressed only as Mr. Bowen. But how could patients and staff less formally address me? Should I tell them to call me "Bunny," which I preferred? In fact, some social workers did call me that the first summer when I worked as an attendant, and as time went on, many of my other coworkers also called me by my nickname. But officially, I was called "Mr. Bowen" as per the custom among the employees of Whitfield, and that became my name for those who did not want to call me Bunny. Others decided to just call me "Bowen."

It was not until 1976 that I worked with a nurse who did not want to call me "Mr. Bowen," "Bowen," or "Bunny." She renamed me "Bo" for "Bowen," which is the name I have adopted since that time. However, to this day, there are former employees of Whitfield who still call me "Bunny" or "Bowen." I had a name tag that had my full name: Ernest L. Bowen III. I believe that tag was made to humor or embarrass me. I never wore it.

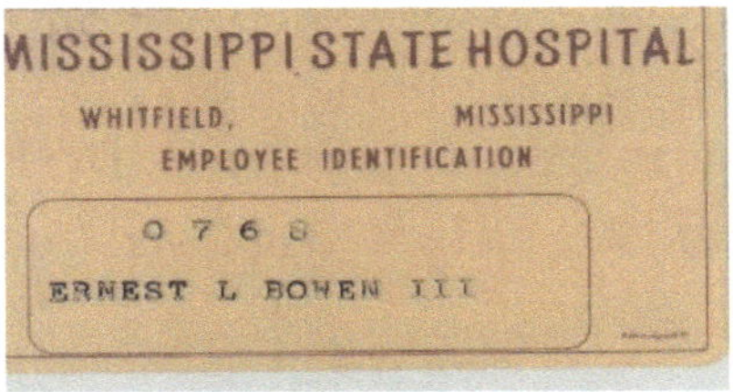

Maximum Security for the Criminally Insane

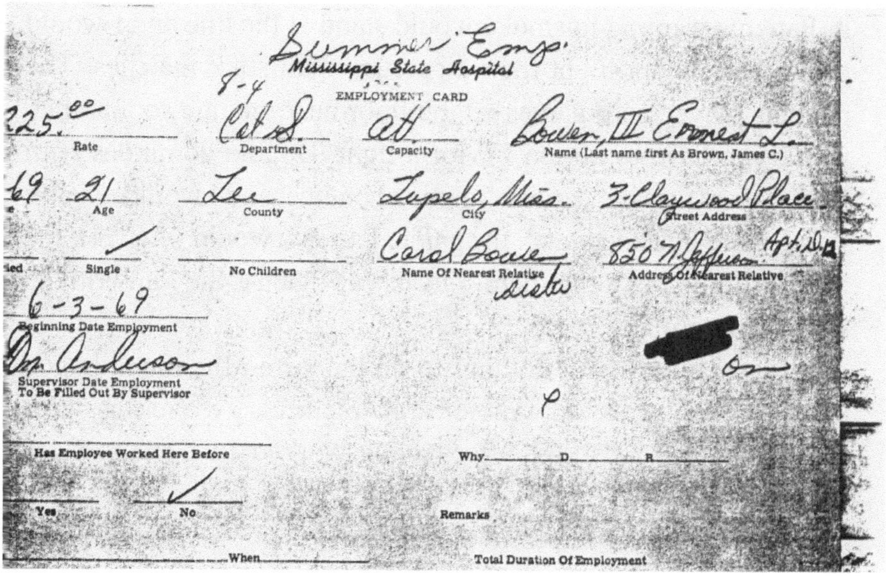

Summer Emp.
Mississippi State Hospital
8-4
EMPLOYMENT CARD

225.00 — Rate
Cot S. — Department
att — Capacity
Bower, III Ernest L. — Name (Last name first As Brown, James C.)

69 — 21 — Age
Lee — County
Tupelo, Miss. — City
3-Claywood Place — Street Address

Single ✓
No Children
Carol Bowe, sister — Name Of Nearest Relative
850 N. Jefferson Apt. D — Address Of Nearest Relative

6-3-69
Beginning Date Employment

Dr. Anderson
Supervisor Date Employment
To Be Filled Out By Supervisor

[redacted]

Has Employee Worked Here Before
Yes — No ✓
When
Why — D — R
Remarks
Total Duration Of Employment

Summer Employment Card

On June 2, 1969, I started work as an attendant in Cottage S (Security). This Maximum-Security for the Criminally Insane building was constructed in 1956 and designed like a prison unit for eighty patients. Dr. Glenn Anderson, Forensic Psychiatrist, was my supervisor. Entrance to the building required going through several locked gates and doors – a process that was quite intimidating for someone who had never seen or been in a jail or prison. There was an observation ward for patients who were admitted for pre-trial evaluation, and there were three wards for the chronic or long-term patients. Patients were classified not by diagnosis but by how well they functioned. The day room had a television set bolted to the wall and metal benches bolted to the floor. Behind the door leading into the day room was a glass observation room rising several feet overlooking the day room and staffed by guards who controlled who could enter and leave the building. Employees who entered the building had no way to exit without the guards unlocking the doors and gates.

The day room had a red line painted across the floor, dividing the patients from the two attendants who sat across from it. Patients wanting to smoke would stand at the line and I would go to the line and light their cigarettes with stick matches. The patients played card games on the floor near the line so that they would not have to go too far for a light. Double dominoes with four players was the patients' game of choice, and I would usually stand at the line and watch the game. Patients would often ask me to play dominoes with them, but it was against the "unwritten" rules to fraternize.

Many times, with nothing to do but sit on the metal bench and "observe," I would write or draw pictures. I wrote this short epistle on June 23, 1969, after having worked on Cottage S for only three weeks.

As I sit here confined in these yellowed
walls of insanity, bleeding with sweat
and discouragement, I see the time
slowly dripping from the big sweep arm
of the clock, outside the locked door.
My patience is growing thin, and weary.
Admissions of solitude creak upon my eyelids.
If only it would snow. If only the rain
could break away from the distant sky
to wet the taste buds of the dust which
brought us here. If only I could get the
Hell out'a here.
6-23-69

I made the decision to push my luck with the rules and sat down on the floor (on my side of the line) and played dominoes with the patients. The issue was first, I should not have been sitting on the floor, and second, my hand went across the line on the patient's side. I took that chance because a tall, Black patient named Roosevelt C., who played dominoes, told me, as the other patients had, that nothing was going to happen to me if I played with them. I played a round of dominoes, and the staff reported me to my supervisor, Dr. Glen Anderson, Forensic Psychiatrist at Maximum-Security. I had only met him once when I first started to work in the building, so I was concerned I might lose my job.

He told me I had broken the rules and that I was not to fraternize with the patients. I argued my case that the patients whom I had gotten to know said they would protect me and that nothing would happen to me. Also, there were guards in the observation room and one in the day room who could clearly see everything that was taking place.

I explained to Dr. Anderson that the patients had little interaction with staff other than our lighting their cigarettes and our sitting on the metal bench. I asked him if he would consider allowing me to interact with the patients. Dr. Anderson agreed and allowed me to continue sitting on the floor and playing cards and dominoes.

I was the first attendant given permission to take part in patient activities in Cottage S. I was assigned to Dr. Anderson's Female back service and Female Receiving after I was hired as a social worker in 1972.

Roosevelt C.

Roosevelt, a patient in Maximum Security, was soft-spoken, well-mannered, and popular with the other patients. I saw him every day in the day room and played dominoes with him and two other patients. I believe he was committed to Whitfield after having murdered someone and was admitted to Cottage S to remain until he could be considered sane enough to stand trial. That was not going to happen on my watch. I never saw him act inappropriately, or manically, or delusional.

Guard Duty

The only time I remember truly "guarding" a patient outside of Maximum-Security was when I was sitting with a patient who was in the general hospital for a minor medical condition workup. An attendant was required to stay in the room with him twenty-four hours a day, but he was not dangerous to himself or others. Henry C. was 75 years old and could not walk without assistance. But I "guarded" him.

Bored and Doodling in General Hospital

Kitchen Duty

All meals were delivered to Cottage S from the Whitfield patient kitchen. Cottage S patients dished up the food and served the meals on trays with plastic plates, plastic cups, and a metal spoon. As done in prisons and jails, all spoons were counted by the attendants before and after each meal. One of my responsibilities was making sure all the spoons were accounted for and returned to the kitchen.

Cottage S. Photo by Bo Bowen

Room Searches

We conducted frequent room searches for illegal contraband that was usually found stuffed in mattresses or between the bed springs. We would sometimes find pieces of metal, wire, and nails with the patient's bedding. Knowing that these items were weapons certainly concerned me, but room searches were conducted by additional security guards.

Maximum Security had an outdoor recreation area surrounded by brick walls with security fencing behind the walls. Small groups of patients were allowed outside where they could sit and smoke or walk the perimeter. The ground was worn down from being walked upon, and some patients could be seen walking along the path several times before it was time to go back in. There was a bench for the attendants to sit on, and there was a guard at the door to allow reentry to the building. I remember a small, bald-headed Black man who quickly walked the path. He would not speak to anyone, and I was warned by both employees and patients that we were not to turn our backs on him. We were not to approach him from behind as he could quickly become disturbed and attack. I heeded that advice.

Summer Ended. Now What?

My summer employment ended on August 27, 1969, but I was not ready to return to college because I still did not know what I wanted to major in, and there was no occupation that interested me. I spoke with Ms. Evelyn Ayres, Nursing Supervisor, and asked if I could stay on for a little longer until I could decide what I wanted to do with my life. She approved my request and gave me a few days off so that I could go home and break the news to my family. That did not go well. I told my parents that this is what I wanted to do and would continue this work until I could figure out the path I wanted to take. I was cut off financially. I was now an official college dropout with no financial support! I was on my own! My parents were still not happy with my decision, but my mother did mail me a few dollars periodically if she thought my father would not find out.

One of the problems hanging over my head was that my college deferment for the selective service draft would no longer apply since I was no longer enrolled in college. Mississippi State was quick on the trigger to notify the draft board. I decided to take my chances, hoping that I would not be called up. My deferment changed from 2-S (college) to 1-A, meaning I was eligible to be inducted into the military. I was on my own with no family support. Because my dad knew the clerk at the Selective Service office, she agreed to give my dad a heads-up if my number was coming up.

MSH 1969-1970 – A Full-Time Employee

I reported to the Male Receiving building on September 3, 1969, in the same position as an attendant and with the same $225 a month pay. I moved out of the men's dormitory and rented an apartment in Jackson with a boyhood friend from Tupelo. He was a student at Millsaps, and both of us could barely pay the rent, much less afford decent food. A packet of Kool-Aid and a box of macaroni and cheese were about as much as we could spend on food.

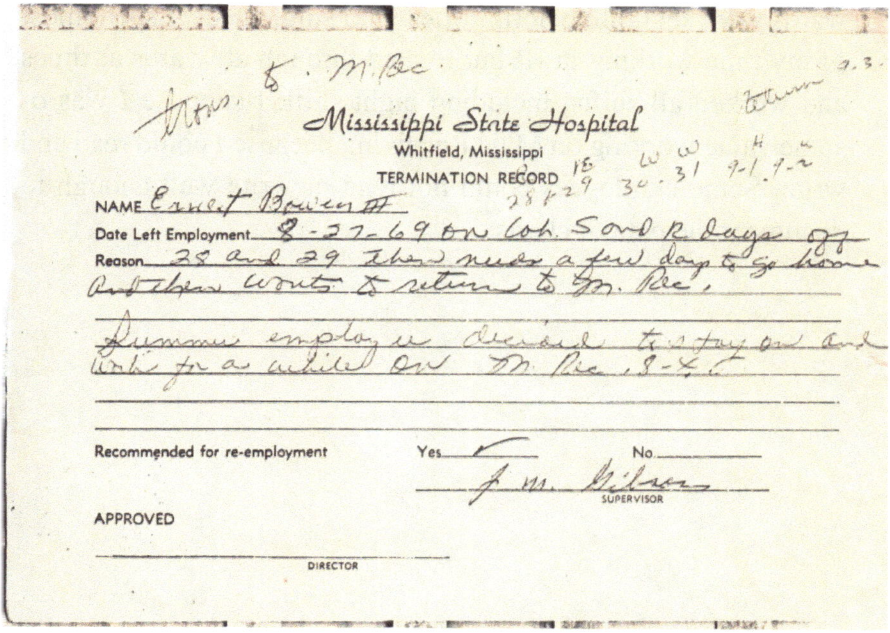

Mississippi State Hospital
Whitfield, Mississippi
TERMINATION RECORD

NAME Ernest Bowen III

Date Left Employment 8-27-69 on Coh. S and R. days off

Reason 28 and 29 then needs a few days to go home and then wants to return to M. Rec.

Summer employee decided to stay on and work for a while on M. Rec.

Recommended for re-employment Yes ✓ No

J. M. Gilson
SUPERVISOR

APPROVED

DIRECTOR

Termination Record

Male Receiving Building #23

The Male Receiving building was the admission building for all male patients except those with criminal charges, who were admitted to Cottage S. There were three wards in the building, and patients were assigned to a ward based on their condition.

Receiving I was called “Hydro” for hydrotherapy. It was a small ward for patients receiving electroshock treatments, those who needed restraints, those who were in delirium tremens, or those who were considered dangerous, requiring constant observation. There were two locked cells with wire-framed doors used for unruly or dangerous patients.

Receiving Wards II and III were the wards for incoming patients. It was in these wards that the physicians would first meet the patients, prescribe medications, and take care of any general medical conditions. Receiving III was on the ground floor and housed the kitchen where all patients would have their meals. The wards were set up like dormitories with single beds. I spent most of my time working in III but rotated through all wards at times and worked all shifts, including night shift. I suppose I was of some value working on Male Receiving because I could read and write. Some employees could not read or write well enough to document the patient charts.

Charles Gordon, a patient in Male Receiving in 1948, sketched this drawing of his ward. Gordon was a long-time reporter for the *Clarion-Ledger* and was admitted to Whitfield for his alcohol problem. He penned his experience at Whitfield in a manuscript titled "Nine Days in a Nut House."

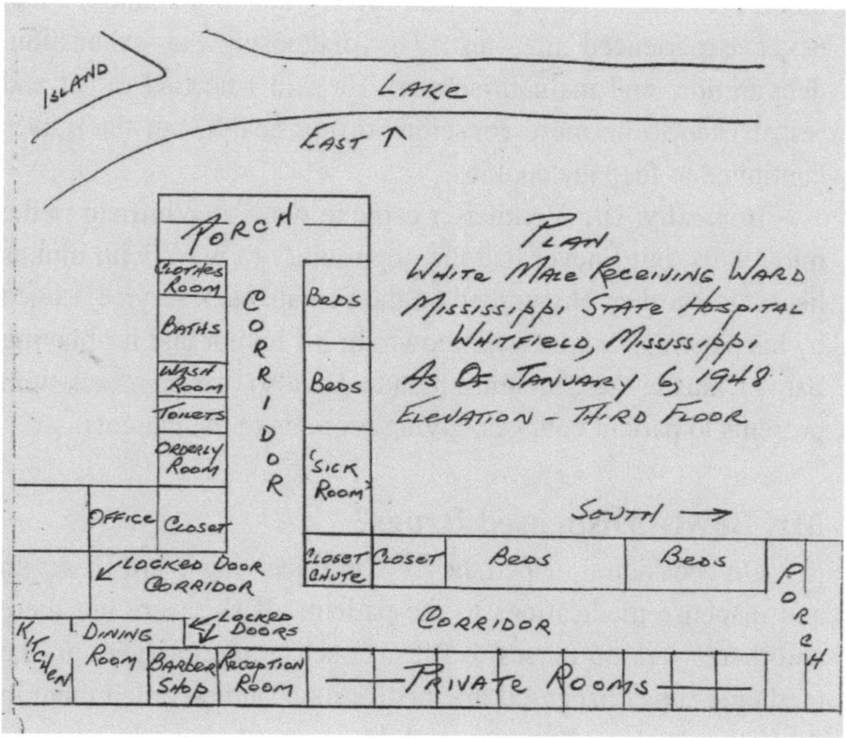

Charles Gordon Male Receiving Sketch. Courtesy of Mac Gordon.

Nurses Linda Manska and Dawn Driskell

I will forever be indebted to Linda Manska and Dawn Driskell, RNs on Male Receiving. But I don't think they knew how I felt about them. There were times I did not have money to eat before my morning shift, and I would come to work hungry. I was not eating properly and stayed light-headed much of the time, especially in the mornings. I had a cafeteria meal ticket (35 cents a meal), so lunch was a given. Linda and Dawn took pity on me and brought me cookies and muffins in the morning when I came in for my shift. They would check my blood pressure and pulse and tell me when I needed to get a checkup. I ended up going to Dr. Ed Werkheiser, who had an office on Jefferson St. near my apartment on Keener Ave. I remember he checked my blood pressure using the cuff on my leg above the ankle. I had never experienced that test. His diagnosis was exhaustion, dehydration, and malnourishment. He said I needed to eat and rest. I tried to be more conscious of my health, but the nurses continued to feed me cookies.

Ironically, Dr. Werkheiser came to work at Whitfield in the mid-1970s, but I never had the opportunity to work with him as his social worker. He worked on the Female back service. Loved by his patients, he was well known for his humor and for playing Santa Claus in the Christmas parade. He also carried a sack with presents to patient cottages, giving presents to the patients.

Mr. Bowen Dispensed Drugs?

On occasion, I helped the LPN in Receiving Ward III set up and dispense medications to the patients. If she were not there and there were no nurses to fill in, I set up the medicine in the medicine cups, dispensed the medications, and recorded them in the patient's chart. Experimental drugs were being administered during that time, so there would be drugs set aside with labels that had only combined numbers and letters to identify them. I never knew the names of these drugs or if they were ever manufactured, but I dispensed them as required.

It was not until 1975, during a state government Performance Evaluation and Expenditure Review (PEER) investigation at Whitfield, that it was discovered that attendants were dispensing drugs. The problem was that there were not enough nurses employed at the hospital. A lawsuit by Attorney David Seth Michaels was brought against the hospital to stop the practice of non-medical staff dispensing drugs. He contacted the Attorney

General's office and the Mississippi Nurses' Association for support in stopping the practice. I can only assume that this practice of attendants dispensing drugs continued from my time as an attendant from 1969-1970 till 1975.

In Dr. William Parker's document "Believe It or Not," he remembered that "patient runners delivered medications to the buildings, often having several thousand pill bottles of Mellaril or Thorazine in their possession at any one time. There was never any difficulty with any of this medication disappearing."[11]

Charge Attendant

On evening shifts, I was considered the charge attendant but not by title. I worked all shifts, recorded the medications, wrote notes in the patient records, made rounds on the three wards, and helped the other attendants in the other wards when needed. I typically would turn the lights out in the wards and make rounds throughout the night.

God, Are You Listening?

I remember a patient who would not stay in his bed at night but would come out into the hall and tell me that God had told him to get out of bed. I would assure him that it was ok to go back to bed and that he was dreaming. After several more times of his coming out into the hall saying that God had talked to him, I cupped my ear like I was hearing something and told him that I had just heard from God and that God wanted me to tell him that it was now OK to go back to bed. He would go back to bed and not come back out the rest of the night. Yes, I know I should not have played into his auditory hallucination, but I knew of no other way to stop him from rising from bed.

Ms. Annie Roby

Ms. Roby was the housekeeping employee for Male Receiving and was always available to help other staff who needed an extra hand. As the housekeeper, she mopped the floors, collected garbage, and changed out all the linens. However, she did not work in the Hydro Ward. That work was left to the male attendants. Ms. Roby was a diligent worker, always had a smile on her face, and was extremely kind to the patients and staff, and me. I believe she was married to another employee at the hospital, and they lived in Pearl.

One time, there was a manic-depressive patient who was quite likable when he was in his manic phase. Because he was always willing to work on the ward, Ms. Roby and I would let him mop the floors, which he did willingly and quickly. Since he worked so fast, we sometimes would have to get him to go back over the floors. He didn't stay in the ward long, so we lost a good worker.

I learned that in 1977, Ms. Roby graduated from a 16-week Nurse Aide-Psychiatric Aide course at the hospital. I didn't know a more deserving employee.

The Kitchen

If I remember correctly, there were no meals brought over from the patient kitchen to Male Receiving on Sunday evenings. There would, however, be sandwiches, cheese, and tea in the kitchen. The cheese was in a round wooden container. I was told that it was commodity cheese provided to state hospitals and programs that served the poor and needy. Ms. Roby had keys to the kitchen, and she would open it up for us to make a sandwich or have a slice of cheese.

Into the Tunnels

There were times patients would slip out of the Male Receiving building, as well as other cottages at the hospital, and one of the first places we looked for them was in the basement tunnels. The tunnels connected all the buildings and were equipped with water, heating, wiring, and lights. A person could go from one building to another through these tunnels. They were constructed of concrete and built by prisoners from the old Rankin County Prison Farm in the mid-1920s. Several times I went down into the tunnels below the Male Receiving building to look for patients who had slipped away from the wards or to search for stashed alcohol. I remember discovering blankets and pillows in the tunnel where a patient had been hiding out. Going into the tunnels was not for the weak-hearted, at least not for me. The tunnels were cold, wet, and sometimes dimly lit. I never knew what I might walk up on.

Fred Chaney, a long-time patient at Whitfield, whose biography I've written, was caught in a compromising position several times with female patients in the tunnels. He also used the tunnel passageways to break into a female patient's cottage, and once made it to the drug room, where he stole drugs. It was reported that he had stolen an electrician's keys when he was helping the electrician.

Nursing Lectures

I asked Ms. Ayers, Director of Nursing, if I could attend the nursing lectures at the student nursing dorm in Whitfield. Psychiatrists regularly lectured to the nursing students who came from St. Dominic, Baptist, and the University of Mississippi Nursing Schools. These student nurses worked all over the hospital, assisting the staff nurses with their assigned patients. Ms. Ayres allowed me to attend the lectures and sit in the back row of the classroom to listen and observe only. I was given time off during my shift to attend these weekly lectures. What I learned from these lectures aided me in understanding more about mental illnesses and medications. I also had the opportunity to socialize with the student nurses. Ms. Ayers, aware of my wandering eye, told me not to fraternize with the nurses. One other point Ms. Ayers made was wanting me to shave off my Fu Manchu moustache. She said it looked like the rear end of a horse. I kept the moustache.

Hydrotherapy (Hydro) Ward – Electroshock Treatments

Even though I was assigned to the other Male Receiving wards, I sometimes worked shifts in the Hydro Ward. Sometimes I would temporarily replace an employee who needed to leave the ward. Or I would be assigned for a shift. Weekends were the worst since there were fewer staff available on all the shifts. There were two locked cells in Hydro for disturbed and dangerous patients. Both were small rooms with steel-meshed doors. There was no pass-through for meals, so the doors had to be unlocked to provide the meals and medication. This was usually a dangerous time, and more attendants were needed in case of disturbance.

Electro-shock treatments were ordered for patients on the Hydro Ward or from other wards in the Male Receiving building. I often helped with electroshock treatments, an experience I will never forget. The treatments were prescribed for several reasons and for different diagnoses. I remember psychotic patients diagnosed with catatonic schizophrenia and bipolar depression receiving shock treatments two to three times a week. I don't remember many male patients receiving shock treatments just for depression. However, shock treatments were often administered for unacceptable behavior. There were times when I witnessed hostile or aggressive patients undergoing shock treatments only because of their behavior. Some received treatments for trying to escape or for assaulting a patient or an employee. The therapy could easily be considered as punishment under certain circumstances, but it could also reduce aggression. Patients often received shock treatments against their will. No patients voluntarily requested shock treatments.

The shock treatments were administered on a gurney with the patient lying on the gurney, sometimes being forcefully held down by the attendants. The patient was given no muscle relaxant or general anesthesia prior to the treatment and, therefore, experienced the full force of the shock. I had read that the hospital could not afford to pay for anesthesia or any relaxant drugs at that time.

One attendant would cup his hands on the patient's heels to keep his feet from hitting the gurney, and there would be one attendant on each side of the patient. We would keep our hands resting on the patient to keep him from falling off the gurney or from trying to escape. However, there were times when a patient was manhandled and held down by force on the gurney, for instance, when he was called for his treatment, or when he would try to hide or put up resistance. On one occasion, when the patient was called, he answered that he was in the bathroom and couldn't come out. One of the attendants went into the bathroom and dragged the man off the toilet while he was having a bowel movement. He was pulled across the floor by his arms and left a trail of feces from the bathroom. We had to pick the man up, place him on the gurney, and hold him down for his treatment. It was not pleasant.

A physician would place a rubber mouth guard in the patient's mouth to keep him from biting his tongue. If a patient fought and resisted the mouth guard being placed in his mouth, he would receive the shock treatment without it. The physician would stand in front of the patient's head and would place the electrodes at the temples. The device looked like a pair of headphones with electrodes on each side. A lubricant that I understood helped in the conduction of the electric current was applied to the device. The black box, as it was sometimes called, would be set for a specific number of seconds, and the voltage would be set. The electric current was supposed to stimulate a person's brain to induce a seizure that could last 30-45 seconds. While the physician held the headset on the patient's temples, he pushed the button on the machine. The patient would immediately have contractions and a convulsion for what seemed an eternity. The attendants would help keep the patient on the table and remain with him until he recovered from the convulsions. He would then be placed on a bed until he started coming out of the shock treatment. The main problem I saw with some patients was confusion and memory loss. Two to three treatments a week could sometimes wreak havoc on both employees and patients. The confusion and memory loss sometimes created agitation, which had to be controlled by physical force.

Shock treatments were found to treat clinically depressed individuals with some degree of success. They were controversial, however, because it was not unusual for a patient to have a dislocated shoulder, fractures of arms and legs, or broken hips. I vividly remember two patients undergoing their treatment when I was assisting. One man was having his first treatment and broke his hip. We heard the break but could not send him to the general hospital until he came out of the convulsion. Another patient dislocated his shoulder, and at the end of his seizure, the physician popped it back in place. To hear a bone snap during an electroshock treatment is an unforgettable memory.

I will never forget Leonard Johnson, a young Black man who was the principal Hydro attendant. Not too tall, he was a scrappy, thin man who always dressed in a white uniform. But was he ever a force to be reckoned with for his response to disturbed and confused patients! This incredibly strong man was the go-to person to stop a fight or restrain a patient. But he was also caring, helpful, and patient with the men in Hydro. At the end of his shift, his white uniform could be torn or splattered with blood. I know this well because there were many a day I would go home with a torn, bloody shirt, scratches, bruises, and sore muscles.

Two articles I read about electroshock treatments surprised me. In one, a team of Italian physicians devised a method that they tested on dogs, which would induce a seizure more quickly with fewer side effects. They inserted one electrode in the mouth and another in the anus, but after seeing that this method tended to induce cardiac arrest, they refined their procedure to focus on the electrical current cranially.

In 1938, their first human trial was on a schizophrenic man who was wandering around a train station in Rome. They applied 110 volts of alternating current for 0.2 seconds bilaterally on his cranium, inducing a seizure. After ten more treatments, they were able to return him home to his wife and job.[12]

Watch Your Back!

I remember vividly, even to this day, when I was working in the Hydro Ward. I was the only attendant on my shift, which was not unusual during the weekends. It was a quiet day with several patients who had had shock treatments the day before and were still in a confused state. The office next to the ward's locked door was very small. A desk and chair faced the wall with a couch behind the desk chair. There was a small supply closet in the office.

The patients in the ward had already had their morning medicines and breakfast. A patient in his late forties who had recently had a shock treatment was sitting on the couch. When this patient was younger, he was said to have had a prefrontal lobotomy. He was napping on the couch, causing no problems.

A large man, well over six feet tall and well over three hundred pounds, in his early fifties, had also had shock treatments the day before and was pacing around the ward. I had been talking to him about resting, but he continued to walk. I was sitting in the office when he came up behind me, grabbed a pencil from a pencil holder, placed his arm around my neck in a chokehold, and with the other hand stuck the pencil in my neck. His whole body was shaking while he had me in the choke hold. He said he was leaving, and somehow, I was able to whisper to him that he could have the ward key and keys to my car, which was parked outside the building. I pulled the keys out of my pocket and gave them to him, but he didn't go to unlock the door. He was extremely excited by this time, and I really felt like I was about to be strangled to death as his grip around my neck was getting tighter. He kept the pencil to my neck but would put it down on the desk occasionally. He didn't see that I had broken the pencil in half. As he grabbed another pencil, I decided I needed to limit the number of weapons he could use. I reached into the pencil holder and started breaking each of the pencils into smaller pieces.

I kept trying to get him to open the door with my ward key, but he was so confused, he just stayed in the office with a stranglehold on me. I can't remember who, but an employee was unlocking the door to come into the ward, and when he did, the patient dragged me to the door and yelled out that he was going to kill me if they tried to come in. I could hear more employees outside the door and tried to tell them that he was serious and that he had me in a stranglehold with a pencil to my neck. I heard Dr. Robert Ritter, the forensic psychiatrist at Maximum Security outside the door, trying to talk to the patient and trying to get him angry enough to come outside the door. The patient was getting angrier, but only towards me, and I yelled out for Dr. Ritter to stop angering him.

The patient continued to say he was going to kill me if they unlocked the door. After what seemed like an eternity, someone unlocked the door to come in, and as soon as the door opened, the patient held me up by his arm. I stuck my foot in the door opening, trying to hold it open as the patient was trying to keep the door closed. I was able to use both feet to push us away from the door so the employees could get in. I pushed so hard that the patient and I stumbled backward immediately. Then, what seemed like a dozen employees were all over him, Dr. Ritter gave him a sedative, and he and others prepared to give him a shock treatment. I was now outside the door while all of this was going on, but they were able to manhandle this large, strong man and push him into one of the lock-up cells. I believe he was transferred to Maximum Security because of this incident. A week or so later, he was transferred back to Hydro, having no knowledge of what he had done. He did not recognize me, and that was fine with me.

I was pretty shaken up. Dr. Ritter told me the hospital was going to reward me for my courage. While the proclamation was well-intended, I never saw the financial reward. Dr. Ritter sent me home and told me to come back to work after the weekend. There was one good thing that came about from this incident. A rule was made that there always had to be two attendants on duty on the Hydro Ward.

I wish this were the end of the story about the patient's attack, but far from it. I began having nightmares, trouble concentrating, and a fear of someone slipping up behind me. Dr. Charles Bell, a psychiatrist, saw that I was having problems and said I could come talk to him. When I started seeing Dr. Bell in his office, he decided that I needed medication for depression. He prescribed Etrafon Forte to treat me for my depression and anxiety, which I took three times a day. I experienced drowsiness and dry mouth routinely and continued to have difficulty concentrating. If other employees were aware I was taking medication because of the Hydro incident, I was not aware of it. Dr. Bell saved me, and I continued to talk with him up until the day I resigned in September 1970 to return to Mississippi State. I continued taking this medication for a very long time and told my professors that I was taking medication that would make me drowsy if I fell asleep in class.

I called Dr. Bell periodically to let him know how I was doing, and he gradually reduced my dosage and finally said that I could stop taking it, but that I could still call him if needed. To this day, I remain fully aware of my surroundings, and I always sit with my back to a wall.

Last Days at Whitfield

I had befriended several social workers at Whitfield who took an interest in me. I would talk to them when they made their rounds in Male Receiving and watched how they interacted with the patients and the doctors. I saw in them patience, professionalism, and concern for their patients. I watched them take notes, and I watched their interactions with the patients and the doctors. I told them that I was interested in their work and asked what I should do. I met with Ms. Kathryn Guice, Social Service Director, whom I had already met and talked with in passing. She took an interest in my desire and talked to me about coming back to Whitfield and being employed as a social worker. I believe the social workers I had met may have talked to her about employing me as a social worker. Ms. Guice said if I went back to college and got a degree, she would hire me when I graduated.

I was ecstatic about coming back to Whitfield. I had fallen for that old hospital and knew that I had more work to do there, but in a more focused position with the education that would enable me to do more for the patients and the hospital. The agreement about getting my degree was augmented by social workers Mary Belle McDonald and Paul Jent whom I befriended and from whom I had sought advice. They and many other social workers and Ms. Guice called me by my nickname, "Bunny." Mary Belle said that she would be writing to me at college and seeing how I was doing with my studies, which she did. Each letter was reinforced by Ms. Guice’s declaration for me to make my grades, graduate, and come to work for her. She didn’t mention cutting my hair.

Back to Mississippi State – One More Time, 1970-1972

It was time to go home and tell my parents what I wanted to do and ask if they would let me re-enroll. They agreed with one stipulation. I had to shave off my facial hair and get a haircut. That meant getting rid of the beard I was growing and cutting my hair to a "reasonable length." I enrolled as a first-semester junior since being on academic probation had kept me back on the low end of my degree. If everything had fallen into place when I first enrolled at Mississippi State in 1966, I would have graduated in 1970, but here I was applying for admission in 1970, starting all over.

I enrolled in the Liberal Arts College and signed up for psychology courses, which I thought would be more interesting than social work courses. I was considering becoming a clinical psychologist. But there was a roadblock. I knew that to get a degree in psychology, I would first have to take a foreign language. Spanish sounded better than French. "Merida."

At Tupelo High School, I had opted not to take a language, which was a mistake. My first day in Spanish Lab, I was greeted by the Spanish instructor in her native language. I had no clue what she was saying. I was directed to a small cubicle with a monitor and headphones. She started speaking in Spanish and I could hear the other students eagerly speaking and responding in fluent Spanish. I was completely lost and knew I had made a grave mistake. At the break, I told her I was better speaking in a rural North Mississippi accent and subsequently dropped the course. The next day, I went back to my advisor and told him I was changing my major again. This time, I went to the School of Education and planned to work towards a BS degree in Educational Psychology, which would have been the closest I could get to being a clinical psychologist. The reward was that I did not have to take a foreign language. But since I would have a minor in history, my advisor wanted me to teach and tried to set me up for practice teaching.

I was able to take elective social work courses and got to know the instructors in the social work department. When one of them asked me why I was taking his courses, I told him that I was going to be a social worker. He clearly told me that only students in the social work department could be social workers. I remember telling him that I had been promised a social work job at Whitfield after I graduated with a degree. At that time, although a social work degree was preferred, many four-year degrees met the requirement. Years later, when I was employed as a social worker, I had the opportunity to train and supervise a social work student from Mississippi State. Her instructor was the same instructor who had told me I could not be a social worker. I got immense pleasure in this because I was to evaluate the student's work and provide a report and a recommendation to the instructor on her social work abilities.

It should be noted that my house address at Mississippi State was "Whitfield" Street in Starkville, Mississippi!

The educational psychology courses I took required a lot of reading and writing discussion papers. In the course, Psychology of Exceptional Children, I wrote observation papers about a child at Whitfield and a child at Southside Elementary School in West Point, Mississippi. These observations were field trips through the Educational Psychology Department at Mississippi State in 1971. I thought it would be interesting to include these papers in this book. My professor was Dr. James Geohagen, who got me over the hurdles. Observation #3 was conducted at Mississippi State Hospital at Whitfield on Male Receiving Ward 2 in 1971. My subject was a 14-year-old boy with emotional problems. Below is my report:

Ernest Bowen
Psy. of Excep Child - 1971

Cont ad

OBSERVATION # 3

The Setting

The setting was Mississippi State Hospital, Male Receiving Ward 2, Whitfield, Mississippi. The ward is locked and is passable only with the key of the personnel. Sleeping quarters, recreational area, cafeteria, and a visiting room are all on the ward. All male patients, regardless of age are brought to this ward for observation and treatment and are released or kept at the hospital for further treatment.

The Child

Michael is a 14 year old white male, approximately 5'5", and weighing around 140 pounds. He wears the regulation hospital clothing—khaki pants, tennis shoes, and an oversized blue denim work shirt. For his size and weight, his clothing is oversized and fits him improperly. At the time I observed him Michael had just taken a bath and was complaining to the attendants that he wanted clothes that would fit and look better on him. His being overweight is a concern with him. His grooming is fair and he has a bad complexion. He is beginning to grow hair on his face and is in need of a shave.

Michael often looks as though he is afraid to touch things of any large size in that he may accidently turn it over. He is very careful of moving chairs and other equipment in the nursing station. He did accidently knock an ash tray on the floor which made him mad.

He walks in a rhythmical fashion prissing from side to side with his feet hitting flatly to the floor. He also has an exaggerated swing motion in his arms letting them go as if they were limp.

Michael's facial expressions are shown at all times. He has a smile on his face and laughs a great deal. His temper flares up a lot and he turns very red in the face. He also has a predominant wrinkle on his forehead when talking.

Michael's speech is in a form of baby talk with a whine and slurring sounds at the end of a statement. The tone of his voice is fairly high and when he gets mad at something he whines louder. When upset, Michael talks faster and his words and phrases are incoherent. He tends to be overemotional. He is angered and frustrated easily and uses profanity loosely. He talks excessively and will continue to talk when the nurses will listen and carry on a conversation with him. He told a male employee an off color joke dealing with sex. He did not seem to be ashamed or embarassed by telling it out loud because I was able to hear it.

Interaction

As far as I can see Michael does not have anyone to run around with except for the attendants and the nurses. He made no attempts to go out of his way to be with other boys, but will when told to. For his size he can not be adequately placed with any particular group. When it came time to clean the ward the head nurse placed him with three of the younger boys. He tried to take over all the responsibilities of the other which left them without anything to do. This situation seems to be the only time he is around other boys his or near his age. He does not appear to be a leader or a follower. He does things his own way without the help of the others. He made it a point to clean in the office first, which is usually done last for the ward duties. He spent more time talking than he did cleaning.

Michael tried to get and keep the attention of the nurses and employees. He went out of his way to please them but they told him to leave the office, he became very angry and hostile towards them. When he was told to help move some boxes down the ward he started talking about going outside. When he was told again Michael began whinning and said that he was the only one who ever did anything on the ward and said that he did not want to do it. At that point he walked away. I was told that when he becomes extremely angry the first thing he will do is burn his clothes or the sheets on his bed. However, when I observed him, all he did was push a smaller boy against the wall and curse him for reasons I did not understand.

Michael is close with the employees. Two or three times he hugged them and put his arms around them. He spends a great deal of time just being around an adult figure. He readily asks for their advice and is somewhat of a nuisance by his never ending questions and comments. This could be seen by the expressions on the faces of the employees.

Michael's activities are limited on the ward and he gets outside on the grounds rarely because of his episodes with setting things on fire. On the ward he sits and watches television when he is not with the employees. He is interested in westerns and cartoon shows. If he has any outside interests, he has not shown any. When he works on the ward he usually mops and cleans the offices. He works in a hurry and he is not very thorough in his tasks. He made a mess of the hall and spilt soap and water on the floor, which he never cleaned up.

As for basic needs Michael enjoys food and drinking cokes. Since I've watched him, he has had very little rest. He is constantly on the go. He attempts to smoke cigarettes when no one is watching- which is against the rules.

Interpretation

Michael seems to have average intelligence and fairly good common sense. He has both social and emotional problems. His lack of pride and self-respect are stumbling blocks in his development. He has no close friends and makes very little attempt to associate with other children. He is at the present time taking psychological tests and has been recently put on a mild tranquilizer to control him better.

Observation #3 - Property of Bo Bowen

The Culture of the State Mental Hospital is a book I chose for an educational psychology class report. I submitted this report to my professor on September 29, 1971:

3203 Ernest Bowen
9.29.71

H. Warren Dunham
S. Kirson Weinberg
The Culture of the State Mental Hospital 284p.

State mental hospitals have been an ever growing medical, social, and moral problem in our complex society. In association with mental illness, the state hospital acts as a custodial department of the State serving society rather than the patient. In such a bold statement as that ther should be evidence instead of rumors and false beliefs. In this report it is not my intention to discredit our state hospital systems. I am merely trying to use the text of The Culture of the State Mental Hospital to explain this phenomenon in such as way as to define the relevant issues as related to social welfare.

I chose this book because I have worked in a mental institute and have seen and experienced the specific routines, relationships with patients, and above all the different cultures in the hospital setting. I assumed before I began reading the book that it would possibly explain unanswered questions I had while working at Whitfield. After reading the book I can safely say that the authors had Mississippi State Hospital in mind when they were observing a typical state mental hospital in Ohio. This only goes to show that state mental hospitals have a traditional core of requirements and that these requirements are handled universally by hospital administrators down to the attendants.

In understanding the problems dealing with social welfare in the state hospitals, it must be noted that those people who cannot afford private counseling and admittance to private hospitals are referred to the state hospital. As defined, social welfare is the "welfare of society, especially of those segments of society that are underpriveleged or disadvantaged because of poverty, poor education, unemployment, etc." As citizens and taxpayers it is our responsibility to see that the hospital's environment must be understood and reorganized if proper therapy is to be achieved.

It is shown that certain traditions which have been established within the state hospital setting impairs both the therapeutic endeavors of the psychiatrists and the progress of the patients toward recovery. By traditions, I refer to the specific cultures of the hospital, such as, the employee culture and the patient culture. The patient lives in a social climate, regardless of the nature of his illness, and by improving this social climate chances for recovery will be increased. The employee culture, in reference to attendants, is usually of the lower class with little education and "no experience necessary" in the treatment of mental patients.

The majority of our society has accepted these traditions with little insight into the problems and policies which are carried out. Social responsibility is everyone's concern , but it is usually left in the hands of those few humanitarians who see the need for change.

The Culture of the State Mental Hospital was a stimulating account of routine custodial care of the mentally ill. Through personal interviews and diagnostic records, the authors attempted to show the nature of emerging cultural norms both of employee and patient in order to evaluate the consequences of their reciprocal influences. The book was straight forward and was easy to comprehend. I would certainly reccommend the book to anyone who is interested in finding out the routines and their effects, in the state hospital setting.

In relating material between the text and courses that I am taking would be a review in itself , but I will try and summarize the relationship. In the required reading of Ideology and Insanity, by Thomas S. Szasz, a psychiatrist, the view of humanistic values is prevalent. Szasz is showing that we tend to regard mental illness and mental hospitals as a myth and we label them accordingly at the expense of the patient. "Psychological and social damage," says Szasz, "often far outweighs the benefits of any psychiatric therapy." The culture of the state hospitals is essentially paralleled in what Szasz is saying, in that mental hospitals help patients recover from personal difficulties by providing room, board, and a medically approved escape from everyday problems He goes on to say that these hospitals relieve people annoyed by the conduct and failings of mentally disturbed people and require that something be done to mental patients and not for them. Therefore this is a social and moral problem and not medical.

There is a correlation between the texts in that the employee culture, referring to the doctors, controls the traditions and practices to the extent that they become concerned with preserving the character of the hospital culture rather than functioning in their professional capacities. The small group of professionals who do retain their therapeutic ideals, regardless of the pressure of the hospital culture, find themselves continually frustrated. The price of release from this frustration is conformity to a rigid social structure and to a fixed routine.

After working a year and a half as an attendant in a mental institute, I can safely say that I have experienced and seen every phase of mental hospital work. As for the employee culture, for which I was a part, the central goal is the complete subjection and control of patients. The culture functions to retain its structure and traditions regardless of practices essential to the therapy and welfare of patients. Going against this culture brought only discontent, harder work, and a general uneasiness with other attendants and professionals who had conformed to the traditions of the hospital.

The patients, despite their psychoses and personal problems, are capable of developing and sustaining a kind of cultural organization within the hospital. The patients' hopes for recovery and going home depend, not necessarily on their particular eccentricities, but on the insight and therapeutic responsibilities of the employee culture.

I an convinced that there is no other way to face these and many other problems in the state mental hospitals unless attention is brought about by concerned citizens, social welfare agencies and legislatures of the particular states, and members of the medical field who will re-evaluate their therapeutic practice.

This report is two-fold in that I broadly evaluated *The Culture of the State Mental Hospital* and that I tried to clarify what I had described as being justifiable observations. There are still many points to consider, such as, apportionments to state hospitals, and yearly wages on a national basis. These do not pretain to the report but are indirectly associated with patient care as reflected through the particular cultures of the state mental hospitals.

A

Before I resigned in 1978, I could see that while there had been many improvements at Whitfield, my 1971 report was pretty much spot on.

Social Service Department

12/6/71

Hi! ——

I told Miss Guice about our Conversation. She said that she was definitely going to hire you if Dr. Jaquith had no objections — & she felt sure that he wouldn't! She told me to tell you to come talk to her one day over the holidays about "the test", etc. So, everything is looking good down here ——

See you real soon
Mary Belk

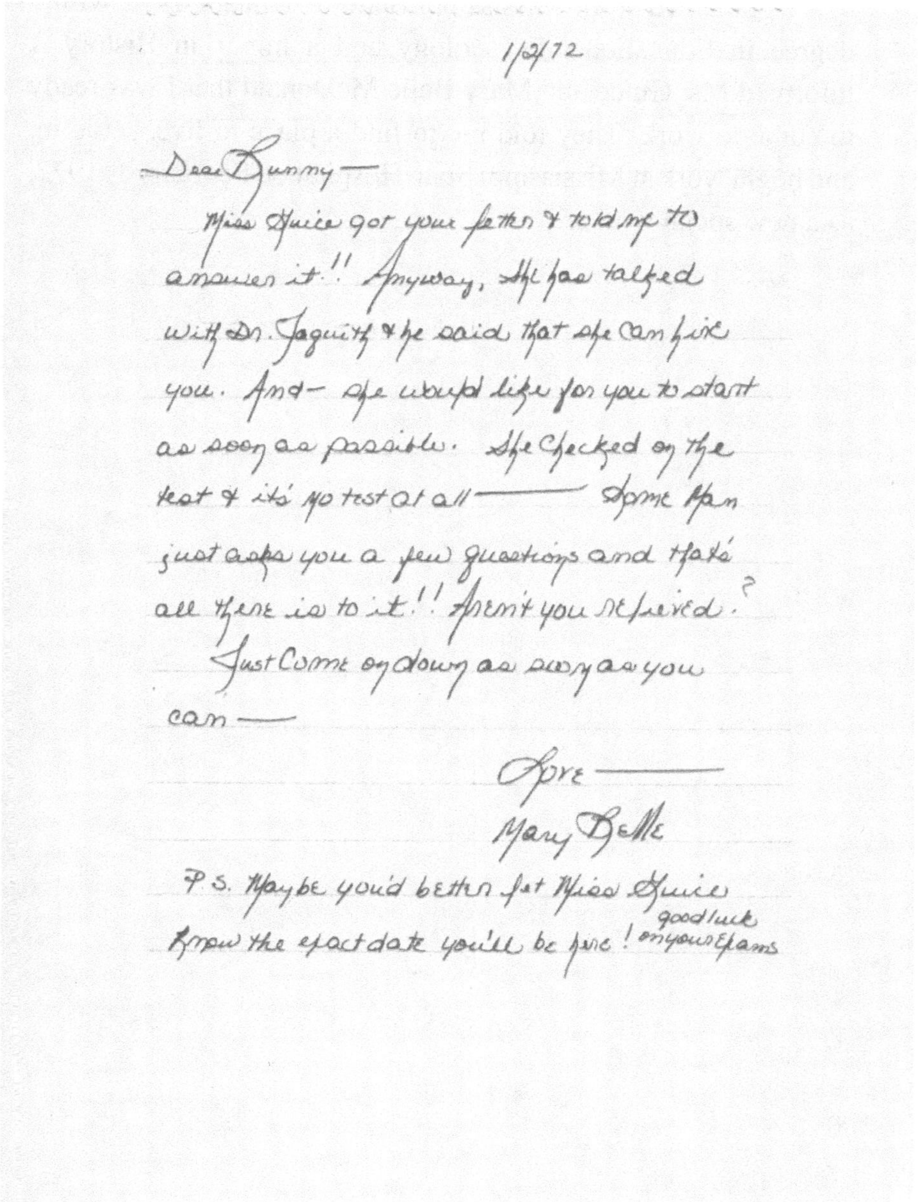
1/2/72

Dear Bunny—

Miss Luice got your letter & told me to answer it!! Anyway, she has talked with Dr. Jaquith & he said that she can hire you. And— she would like for you to start as soon as possible. She checked on the test & it's no test at all—— Some man just asks you a few questions and that's all there is to it!! Aren't you relieved?

Just come on down as soon as you can—

Love——

Mary Belle

P.S. Maybe you'd better let Miss Luice know the exact date you'll be here! good luck on your exams

Mary Belle Letter

Mission Accomplished

I graduated from Mississippi State in January 1972 with a degree in Educational Psychology and a minor in History. I informed Ms. Guice and Mary Belle McDonald that I was ready to come to work. They told me to find a place to live, settle in, and begin work at Mississippi State Hospital on February 1, 1972, as a new social worker.

Mississippi State Hospital 1972-1978

Ms. Kathryn Guice

Ms. Guice, Director of the Social Services Department, was my mentor. She counseled me, helped train me, and gave me opportunities early in my career. She freely gave me personal advice, like not dating people I work with. I ignored that advice, but found later that she was right.

Ms. Guice's Retirement Party. Photo courtesy of Debbie Dunlap.

On good days, she would call me "Bunny." Other days, it was just Mr. Bowen. She would attach notes to my assignments that were usually direct but sometimes funny. One note said I looked like Hawkshaw Hawkins, a country music singer. I am not sure where that came from, but I thought it was funny. She also wanted me to cut my hair, which was long at the time. Ms. Guice always wore her hair up in a bun, except for one time at one of my apartment parties, she and her partner, Arlene, came dressed like beatniks, and she had let her hair down, which fell to below her waist. Ms. Guice retired, and at her retirement party, the staff gave her Amelia Earhart luggage because she and Arlene planned to travel. But shortly after her retirement, she was diagnosed with cancer. Their plans to travel would not happen. I always think of her when I hear of Amelia Earhart's luggage.

Social Work Training

Photo of Bo Bowen, 1974

Mary Belle McDonald and Paul Jent were responsible for supervising, training, and teaching me how to interview patient families for a social history. They taught me how to use a Dictaphone to record my histories. I followed them on their rounds to Male and Female Receiving and to the back service. I had already been in the Maximum Security and Male Receiving buildings, so I felt at home when we made rounds there.

Mary Belle and Paul took me to some of the buildings that housed disturbed patients, so I could understand how to interact with them. Never turning my back on a patient was a lesson I had previously learned the hard way when attacked by a patient in the Hydro Ward. Since that time, wherever I am, I have always chosen to sit with my back to a wall and to try to be aware of the people behind me.

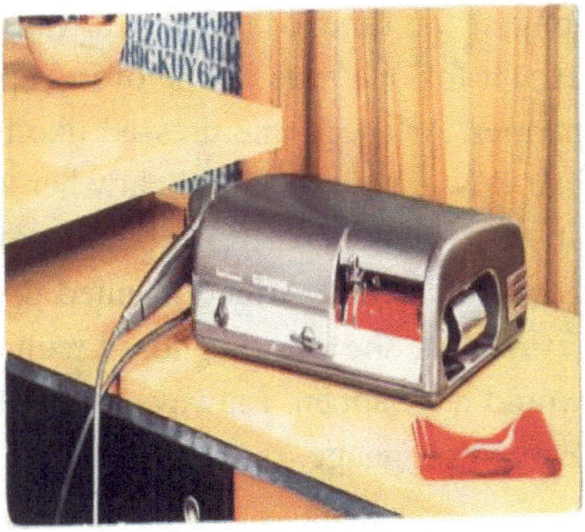

After successfully learning to interview families, I would go over my notes and record the history using a Dictaphone. The notes would be given to someone in the secretarial pool who would painstakingly have to listen to and transcribe the social history. The transcription would be returned to me to review for any errors, and if none appeared, it would be sent to the patient's physician and Medical Records. I often made copies of these social histories so that I could remember vital facts about a patient. Having a microphone in my hand, I could not resist providing a few extra comments, singing a tune, or just talking to the people in Medical Records about nothing. I knew they wouldn't spill the beans about my antics.

Physician Assignments

All social workers were assigned to doctors and their services, whether they were in the receiving buildings, back service, or a combination of both. Whitfield had both general practitioners and psychiatrists on staff. Some of the physicians had no psychiatric training or knowledge of psychiatric drugs and depended on their own research or help from staff psychiatrists. As an example, I was assigned to work with a friend of Dr. William Jaquith, who was the director of the hospital. The physician came from Florida, where he had practiced dermatology and treated the rich ladies who spent too much time on the beach. When he came to work at Whitfield, he turned heads because he sported a Fu Manchu moustache (which I certainly could not argue with), and he wore wooden clogs. His thumping clogs could be heard quite well clunking in the hallways.

Another physician I worked with was an ophthalmologist who had had some psychiatric training. I also worked with a general practice physician who had a good patient manner but gave up on the female patients in Female Receiving. When he thought they were not improving, he would send them to the back service. I thought long and hard about it before I reported his treatment of one of his patients to Dr. Mary Hogan, Chief Psychiatrist in Female Receiving. I hesitated to make the report, but the woman had been on heavy doses of Elavil that made her more depressed than anxious. I researched the Physician Desk Reference (PDR) on the drugs she was taking and found that an excessive dose outside the norm of one of the drugs was causing her problems. Dr. Hogan reviewed the chart, took charge of the patient, and told the physician to place her on a different drug regimen, saving her from a long life on the back service. This was certainly outside my level of expertise, but I took a chance that speaking up was better than the alternative. The physician later had a psychotic breakdown and was relieved of his duties.

Social workers would periodically rotate to the numerous services or be assigned to new doctors who came to work at Whitfield. I experienced working with diverse types of doctors and medical students and dealt with their idiosyncrasies. It seemed to me that Ms. Guice and Mr. Doyce Ward, who later became Social Service Director, assigned me to new physicians – maybe to talk to them about the culture of the hospital? Or maybe because I was used to carrying a large load of patients. Or it may have been some form of tormenting me to work with a new physician who had no psychiatric experience. I gladly took on the assignments.

At one time, I had over nine hundred patients in my caseload because I had taken on additional caseloads from other social workers or staff who were on vacation or who had resigned. I was able to get my work done, but it was not of any benefit to the patients because I could not spend the necessary time with them. Having a case load of this size is certainly unheard of today.

I Was a Jr. Social Worker

When I joined the Social Services staff at Whitfield, I was listed as a "Social Worker." In late 1972, there was a reclassification of staff, and anyone who had a social work degree would now become "Institutional Social Worker I" and would receive a salary increase. Because my degree was in educational psychology, I no longer qualified for the classification. Ms. Guice said she would see what she could do through Dr. William Jaquith, now Director of the Hospital, to have me "grandfathered" in since I had been working as a social worker.

In the interim, I added "Jr." to my name badge. Then it said, "Mr. Bowen, Jr., Social Worker." I figured that since I was not "qualified" and did not receive a classification or a raise, my caseload might slow down. It did not decrease, however, and I was very unhappy but could do nothing about it.

My reclassification did go through, though, and on January 1, 1973, I was approved by the Mississippi Classification Commission and Dr. Jaquith. I ended up being grandfathered since I had been working as a social worker without the proper degree. I then removed the "Jr." from my name tag.

Whitfield Admissions 24/7

During the time I worked at Whitfield, admissions were allowed seven days a week, twenty-four hours a day, 365 days a year. Brenda McAdory Brantley was responsible for the admissions office, and Bettie Lee Millis worked at the desk as well. These two ladies were some of my favorites at Whitfield.

Social workers were assigned a weekend shift in the office to interview patient families, handle telephone calls from family members, and perform other duties as needed. We worked alone, and sometimes we would be stacked up with patient families waiting to be interviewed. The admissions office would call and provide us with information that we would use when interviewing family members. They would then send them upstairs to our offices. I would close the office for lunch, but there always seemed to be a family waiting downstairs to see me.

Working the holidays meant interviewing families who had brought a family member in for treatment. I dare say a lot of these admissions were for drugs or alcohol, but I have no proof. Christmas Eve and Christmas Day were considered an acceptable time for a family to drop someone off at the hospital because that relative got drunk and ruined everyone's Christmas.

I was single when I worked at Whitfield, and rotation for the major holidays would sometimes fall on a worker who had already asked for time off to be with their families. My family was in Tupelo, and my sister, even though she lived in Jackson, would often go home for the holidays. Consequently, with no family around, I offered to work the holidays. Although it probably sounded gracious of me, I did not mind working those holidays as I would get other days off. What I missed the most was the traditional family meal. But then the employee cafeteria was open.

Dr. Bill Parker remembered that on weekends, nights, and holidays during the 1970's, there would be one physician and one nurse to cover all 5,063 patients, including patients at Hudspeth Center, in addition to the new patient admissions. The Hudspeth Center was a facility for intellectually and developmentally disabled individuals. Dr. Parker said it was not unusual to admit twenty patients after 3:00 p.m. to the receiving wards.[13] An admission clerk recalled admitting "fifty-four patients in one 24-hour period, which ended on Friday. Eight came in one car."

Signs of Spring

When social workers left one service to rotate to their next assigned one, they were introduced to the patients in that new building. In 1974, Mike Edwards was working with Dr. Bill Parker in Female Building 33, and I was the new social worker introduced to the patients. The building reporter for *The Grapevine*, the patient newspaper, wrote in her column that I would start making rounds with Dr. Parker, and, according to the reporter, I was quoted as saying to her, "Signs of spring are here because the narcissi are blooming and some of the grass is already green." I got a few funny comments from this introduction to Building 33, mainly because I did not know a daffodil from a dandelion. *The Grapevine* was a patient-run newspaper published each month. The staff included an editor, reporters from patient buildings, a typist, general office workers, assemblers, and deliverers.

The Full Moon

Doctors on call during a full moon knew they would be making visits to the Epileptic Cottage because of the number of grand mal seizures that would take place during the night. While there is debate on the connection between epileptic seizures and the lunar cycle, there are still many in healthcare who say there appears to be a connection. Doctors would spend time in the building stitching up patients from their falls and dreading the nights of the full moon. Once, while I was making rounds in the building, a patient had a grand mal seizure, and a patient witnessing the seizure said, "He don't know where he's at." It was not amusing, but he did not understand what was taking place.

How to Use an Electric Razor

I had a patient in the Epilepsy Cottage who was admitted for drinking hydrochloric acid that burned and severely damaged his throat. He wore a cover over his throat to keep it clean. A chemistry student from India at Mississippi State, he had attempted suicide when his girlfriend broke up with him. In the building, he was not allowed to shave for fear that he would try to cut his throat. I brought an electric razor from home and taught him how to use it. Getting him to puff out his cheek to shave was an experience because he could barely speak English. And the results of the acid certainly affected his speech. I don't know whatever happened to him.

Buildings #90 and #88

Buildings 90 and 88 were the most deplorable buildings on the campus. They housed disturbed patients who could not be placed anywhere else. One floor had mostly Black patients in cells without beds. There was a hole in the concrete floor for drainage. The wood doors had a hole in them so patients could be observed. The problem was that some of the patients would smear feces in the hole, and staff had to be careful when walking down the halls because some disturbed patients would throw feces out through the hole. Attendants in the building would use hoses to wash down the patients and their cells. Charles Gordon, in his manuscript "Nine Days in a Nut House," described how the patients were treated in the building. He said that a barber would shave the patient's hair to keep vermin or bodily waste off.[14]

Making rounds in this building was most difficult. Meeting and talking with patients about their needs was sometimes fruitless and dangerous. Female social workers typically were told by the physicians to avoid certain floors in the buildings.

Attorney David Seth Michaels filed a lawsuit in 1975 concerning the conditions of the building and the care of the patients. He wanted the building to be condemned and filed numerous lawsuits against the hospital to force the issue. It was meant for the hospital to transfer patients to other buildings. Consequently, building 90 was condemned, and the patients were moved to other buildings. Shortly after the building was condemned and thus closed, social worker Paul Jent, Dr. Emily Eisenhower, who was an M4 from the University of Mississippi Medical Center, and I entered the building. We wanted to see the status of the building after the patients were moved out. It was an eerie feeling to walk through the halls and see the foulness on the walls and floors, paint peeling from the walls, and the disgusting smell. We entered the cells and took photos through the holes in the door of the interior of the cells that were covered in feces.

This photo is not from MSH but an imgur Pinterest JPG file which represents the door and opening in the door we witnessed.

Pinterest JPG File, Imgur

Years later, working for the Division of Medicaid, I had the good fortune to know Dr. Randy Hendrix, Director of the Department of Mental Health. I first met him when he was the director of the North Mississippi Retardation Center, and I was on a team conducting independent assessments of the State's facilities. I thought that Dr. Hendrix would want to see the photos I had taken of Building 90 since he was not the director at the time the building was condemned. I gave the photos to him to review and expected that I would get them back quickly. However, he never returned them, and I had not made copies. Little did I know the Department of Mental Health had been sued by David Seth Michael, who wanted the department's photo evidence admitted in his lawsuit. Dr. Hendrix retired, and I forgot about the photos until I began working on the Fred Chaney biography. I realized then that there were many references to that building, and including those photos would confirm what we all had witnessed.

Hydrotherapy

We also went to the hydrotherapy room on the basement floor of the Male Receiving building. This was before the hospital finally decided to create the MSH Museum and save the equipment. I took pictures of Dr. Eisenhower in the "heat box," which was a marble sauna with light bulbs lining the interior walls and an opening for the head. I also took pictures of her with the hydrotherapy bath sprayers. There was broken marble and seepage of water on the floors.

MSH-14

Mississippi State Hospital
WHITFIELD, MISSISSIPPI
CASE NOTES

Case No.__________
Year No.__________ Name__________

5/25/76

MEMO

TO: MR. JAMES STUBBS, DIRECTOR

FROM: ERNEST BOWEN, SOCIAL WORKER, SOCIAL WORK DEPARTMENT

Re: Hydro-Therapy Equipment

Several months ago I discussed with you the possibility of preserving the Hydro-Therapy Equipment in the basement of Building #23. At the present time some work is being done on the ceiling of the "Hydro-room" but I do not know how much work will be done there. I hope the equipment can be saved because it is a part of this hospital's history.

Anything you can do to preserve the equipment will be appreciated not only by me but many others who are aware of the historical value.

Ernest Bowen, Social Worker
EB/hm

Memo to Mr. Stubbs. Property of Bo Bowen

In 1976, I wrote two memos to Mr. James Stubbs, the new Director of the Hospital, about saving the hydrotherapy equipment. I had already contacted the Mississippi Department of Archives and History to see if they would be interested in the equipment. And they were. The two memos I wrote went nowhere, and if I remember correctly, Mr. Stubbs told me it was not a priority.

, MSH Hydrotherapy Room. Photo courtesy of MSH

Almost twenty-five years later, the hydrotherapy room was saved and turned into a museum. Interestingly, Dr. Henry Boswell's granddaughter, who is also a family friend of mine, was contracted to work with Whitfield to restore the hydrotherapy room and to work with historical documents and memorabilia that tell the story of this therapy and Whitfield. Dr. Boswell was the former director of the TB Sanatorium and worked with Dr. Jaquith on TB treatments at Whitfield. Dr.

Boswell conducted investigations into the care patients received at Whitfield in the 1950s and 1960s and later became the Director of the Mississippi Department of Mental Health.

MISSISSIPPI STATE HOSPITAL

W. L. Jaquith, M.D.
Chief of Medical Staff

WHITFIELD, MISS.
August 3, 1976

James C. Stubbs
Director

MEMO

TO: MR. JAMES STUBBS, DIRECTOR

FROM: ERNEST BOWEN, SOCIAL WORKER, SOCIAL WORK DEPARTMENT

Re: Hydro-Therapy Equipment

Please note attached copy of a Memo sent to you dated 5/25/76 regarding the Hydro-Therapy Equipment in the basement of Building #23.

I would appreciate anything you can do to preserve the equipment and if I can be of any assistance, I will be glad to discuss this with you.

Ernest Bowen, Social Worker
EB/hm

Memo to Mr. Stubs Hydrotherapy

Photo by Bo Bowen

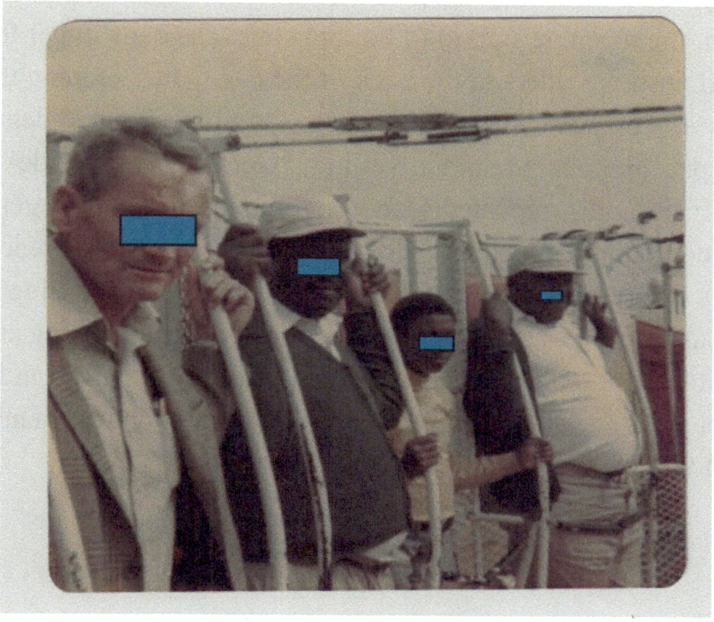

State Fair Photo taken by Bo Bowen

Mississippi State Fair

For decades, male and female patients in the back service made annual trips to the Mississippi State Fair in Jackson. Any patient who wanted to go to the fair would be able to do so with their doctor's approval and the advice of the building attendants. Male and female patients would go separately on different days and were transported to the fair in buses that the hospital rented. The hospital paid for the admissions for all patients, social workers, and building attendants, and for their lunches. Nursing staff also attended in case of an emergency. The excursion to the fair was usually from 11 to 3. If I remember correctly, all the rides were free for the patients.

One vivid memory I have is when social workers Kit Whitsett Fields, Billy McLaurin, Helen Harris, and I took male patients from several back service buildings. On the zero-gravity ride, patients would stand side by side but in a small enclosure with a safety strap across the front of the cage to keep them from falling out. I think only our patients were on this ride. As the ride began, the machine started to tilt and spin. The centrifugal force would push the riders to the back of the cage, thus keeping them in place. However, when the ride began to tilt at about 70 degrees and spin, one patient started yelling, "Get me off this ride. Get me off this ride" repeatedly and then lunged forward to get off the ride. Patients on either side tried to restrain him. Kit reached across one of the patients to help hang onto him. All during this time, as the ride was spinning and tilting, we started yelling at the operator to stop the ride. He eventually stopped the ride, and we all got off. The patient was shaken up, but very soon was thankful that it was over.

MS State Fair Phots by Bo Bowen

Mirror, Mirror on the Wall

Many of the buildings on the back service were always in need of some kind of repair, whether it be plumbing, wiring, heating, or broken appliances. Hospital staff were usually quick to make major repairs, but something as simple as replacing a bathroom mirror went undone. Cleaning supplies, paper products, and towels were often in short supply. I was making my rounds on a male back service building and did a walk-through, inspecting the wards and the bathroom. Propped up in the window was this piece of a mirror that the male patients used when they wanted to comb their hair and shave. I asked why there was no mirror and said that the piece of the glass mirror could be used as a weapon, or that someone could get cut just by handling it. The attendant said that that was all they had and that they had made supply requests for a mirror, but never received one. I took the piece of mirror to the business office and asked that someone in the office order a standard mirror for the building. They agreed, but I had to follow up several times before the mirror arrived. I brought a mirror from home to the cottage until the new one came in.

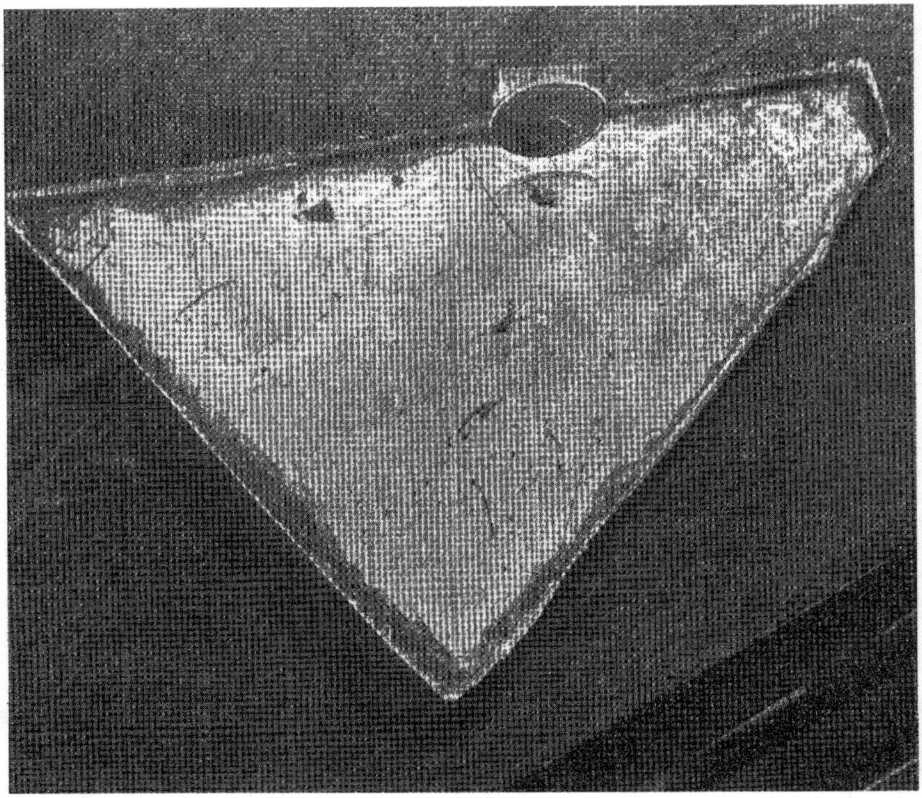

Photo of mirror by Bo Bowen

Dr. Ed Ruff and the "Miracle" of Thorazine?

Dr. Ed Ruff was a psychiatrist in Male Receiving, and I was assigned as his social worker. A young Black man was admitted to the Hydro Ward under a sheriff's escort. He was a very thin but muscular man who had been extremely disturbed and combative while in jail and while on his way to Whitfield. He had already gone through several pairs of handcuffs by pulling them apart. The sheriff's office had put him in leg irons, chains around his waist, and another set of handcuffs. When the patient was placed into a hydro seclusion cell in Male Receiving, he immediately started banging his fists on the steel mesh door. He repeatedly hit the same place on the door until the steel mesh screen began to show the indentation from his fist. He appeared catatonic and did not talk or yell, just stared ahead. Not knowing what to expect, I steered clear of the door he was pounding on. Amazingly, his fist was not bleeding, nor were there any cuts.

Dr. Ruff began giving the patient injections of Thorazine and other anti-psychotic drugs. The patient had to be held down by the attendants while Dr. Ruff administered the Thorazine. He began to tolerate the drugs and began to eat the meals he was provided, but he stayed in the cell. We opened the door and slid his meals to him across the floor. The patient did not threaten staff since he had calmed down, but at the same time, we were leery of his being released into the ward with the other patients.

Dr. Ruff continued increasing doses of Thorazine, which at that time were given in both tablet form and by injection. As I understood it, Thorazine had been widely used at Whitfield since the late 1950s, but in smaller dosages. As Dr. Ruff increased the dosage, the patient began to respond, and there was a breakthrough. Dr. Ruff asked the patient if there was anything he wanted or wanted to do if he were to be let out of the cell. He asked Dr. Ruff if he could go fishing. Staff were concerned that the patient was still dangerous and tried to discourage Dr. Ruff. That did not deter him, however, and he let the patient out of the cell and took him to the lake behind the Male Receiving building. He brought cane fishing poles and crickets, and they fished off the banks of the lake under the watchful eyes of staff. If there was ever a breakthrough with Thorazine, I think this was it. It wasn't a miracle, just a good drug.

The Trucker is on the Road Again

A truck driver hooked on amphetamines was admitted to the Hydro Ward. He was a large man in delirium tremens. Lying in his bed, he thought he was driving his 18-wheeler. He placed his hands in the air as if on a steering wheel, shifted gears, and talked on his CB radio. I was assigned to this patient as his social worker and tried to communicate with him. It was impossible as he was "on the road." The only conversation I remember having with him was asking him what he saw on the road and what gear he was driving in. He vividly described the scenery on the highway as he was shifting gears.

Lieutenant Governor Evelyn Gandy

Lt. Governor Evelyn Gandy and special guests met with hospital administrative staff in observance of National Hospital Week, May 9-15, 1976. According to the May 13, 1976, patient newspaper, *The Grapevine,* Lt. Governor Gandy was the featured speaker at a special luncheon at the hospital. I remember this occasion only because prior to their tour of the Female Receiving building, new furniture and bedding were placed in the ward. It seemed unfortunate that the furniture had not arrived long before this visit when it was needed, rather than arriving in time to impress the Lt. Governor.

"We Don't Eat No Guinea Eggs."

A Black male patient on the back service would repeatedly say, "We don't eat no guinea eggs. We don't eat no guinea eggs." Maybe he had lived on a farm before being admitted to Whitfield. One of the attendants in the building said, "Watch this." She brought out a Bible, turned to Psalm 23:4, handed it to the patient, and asked him to read the passage. He started reciting, "We don't eat no guinea eggs. Yea though I walk through the valley of the shadow of death, we don't eat no guinea eggs."

And What About the Cats?

There were cats all over the hospital. And no mice or squirrels. I do not recall seeing any cats living in the building and would have remembered since I'm allergic to cat fur. Dr. Bill Parker, in his "Believe it or Not" fact sheet about the hospital from the early 1970s to early 1980s, said that there were "900 cats and no squirrels, [and] one patient had a herd of over 100 cats she moved from building to building when she was transferred."[15] Dr. Jaquith said that they had to kill 700 cats, knowing that it would be an issue for the patients. The article said the cats were shot because it would have been much harder to catch them and put them to sleep.[16]

The Alligator Pond

There was a small pond on the west side of the campus, well behind the patient buildings, where some staff would go fishing. There was an alligator in the pond that sometimes ventured out onto the grounds of the hospital. He would be captured and returned to the pond. I never saw the alligator, but believe it was a small one. The story I heard about the feral cats at the hospital was that they would be captured and fed to the alligator. I don't know if that was true, but it was an interesting story. In the early

1940s, the hospital raised hamsters for experimentation. Those creatures would have made any alligator happy.

Rose Hill Cemetery

The Hudspeth Regional Center is a facility for intellectually and developmentally disabled individuals located west of Mississippi State Hospital. The facility is operated through the Department of Mental Health with full support of the State Hospital's resources. It was formally known as the Hudspeth Retardation Center and the Annex. Across from Hudspeth is an archway that leads to the Rose Hill Cemetery, established in 1936 shortly after Whitfield opened its doors in 1935. It is there where patients were buried according to the family's wishes. If, however, relatives refused to make burial arrangements or could not be located by social workers, those patients were also buried here. The hospital chaplain would handle setting the time and date of the service. The hospital's maintenance department would open and close the grave and arrange with the Transportation Office to have six pallbearers to lower the casket at the gravesite. The warehouse was to always keep an adequate supply of caskets in stock.

Rose Hill Cemetery. Photo by Bo Bowen

It was either my lack of attention or my lack of knowledge, but I never knew the cemetery was named Rose Hill, nor do I know the origin of the name Rose Hill. I had only heard the graveyard called "Monkey Hill." It was a name I heard when a patient died, and no relatives could be found. We knew the patient would be buried at "Monkey Hill." Dr. William Jaquith, former director of the hospital, said the graveyard was referred to as "Monkey Hill" by the patients. He was never able to find out where the name came from.[17]

I, too, have no idea how or why the cemetery was known as that, but I remember having a conversation with a member of the hospital staff a few years ago in which I said "Monkey Hill" and was quickly told that name was not to be used.

The Rose Hill Cemetery was a potter's field covering acres of land with over 4,000 burial sites. Prior to the 1960s, concrete markers had only a number to identify the patient, with a record associated with the patient's name and medical record. Many of the markers had sunk into the ground and could no longer be visible. Headstones later were inscribed with the patient's name, date of birth, and date of death. The Friends of the Mississippi State Hospital and the Guardian Angel Project funded headstones for patients who were identified, and non-profit groups helped locate and clean the markers. It is my understanding that the earlier burials are not identified on a graveyard plat book, meaning the names of those hospital patients are unknown.

The Asylum Hill Project

The Mississippi State Lunatic Asylum, later renamed the Mississippi State Insane Asylum, was located on land that is now the University of Mississippi Medical Center (UMMC) in Jackson, Mississippi. The lunatic asylum opened in 1855 and closed in 1935 when the patients were transferred to the newly opened Mississippi State Hospital at Whitfield.

In the early 1970s, while attending a social work meeting at the Jackson Mental Health Center that was once located on the St. Dominic Hospital campus, another social worker and I spied what we thought were headstones across the driveway on the UMMC property. We knew that the asylum had been located on that property, so we crossed over the fence and found dozens of headstones that were falling over, broken, or unreadable. We recorded the names we could read on the headstones and searched medical records at Whitfield to determine if they were patients at the asylum. Most of those people had not been patients at the asylum, but we found a few while searching for their medical records. The history of the asylum has noted that there could have been not only patients of the asylum but veterans of the Civil War and patients from the Asylum Hill Community, which is now the Fondren neighborhood in Jackson.

In 2012, while construction was underway to build a parking lot on the UMMC campus, graves were discovered and unearthed. UMMC officials discovered more than one thousand bodies, which were thought to have been from patients at the Mississippi State Lunatic Asylum. Further surveys and underground radar showed there could be as many as seven thousand graves over twenty acres of the campus. Some grave markers were found, but a large majority of markers were painted wooden stakes that deteriorated over time. Over four thousand death certificates were found at the Mississippi Department of Archives and History. The records determined the date of death and the cause of death, but finding the graves of those patients would be nearly impossible.

The UMMC Asylum Hill Project was created with a diverse group of scholars and researchers to study and exhume the bodies. More information about the Asylum Hill Project and the Asylum Hill Research Consortium can be found at https://asylumhillproject.org.

I attended the first Asylum Hill Consortium on July 20, 2019, and provided the names of those we found at the cemetery across from St. Dominic Hospital. I also had a document about the old Asylum written by Fred Chaney, a patient admitted in 1932, 1933, and 1934. Chaney described the Asylum, the ward where he was kept, the kind of patients he lived with, and his own exploits while institutionalized. I read his description of the Asylum, and my presentation was filmed as part of the Consortium project. I have also written the biography of Fred Chaney, titled "The King of Whitfield."

Whitfield Highball

Constipation was a side effect that patients taking antipsychotics and antidepressants complained about. The go-to concoction for patients who reported constipation was a combination of cascara and milk of magnesia – the "Whitfield Highball." The two, when stirred together, gave the appearance of chocolate milk, which visually made it easier to drink. Or so the patient thought. Cascara, made from the bark of a bush, contains chemicals that stimulate the bowel and have a laxative effect. Milk of magnesia is a laxative mixed with cascara that will produce a fast response. Indeed, sometimes it acted too fast for some patients.

Dr. Bill Parker remembered that 10,000 doses of Pericolase a month were being dispensed in the early seventies, and Milk of Magnesia was purchased by the gallon.[18]

Conversion Disorder or Hysterical Neurosis?

I took a course at Mississippi State about such mental health diagnoses as schizophrenia, manic-depression, and conversion disorder. Conversion disorder, now known as Functional Neurological Disorder (FND), was defined as a mental condition in which a person has physical symptoms that cannot be explained by neurological or medical conditions... (Mayo Clinic)

The second time I heard this diagnosis was when a teenager was admitted to Male Receiving in a wheelchair. He was paralyzed from the waist down and needed staff assistance in most activities. He was assigned to the child psychiatrist on staff, and from what I remember, he was referred to the psychology department for testing. He stayed on the Receiving floor with several other teenagers and seemed to get along well with them. At that time, younger patients were separated as best as could be from the adult patients. It was discovered he had injected mayonnaise into his penis at home, and it was thought the guilt he had from this experiment caused his "paralysis" and his ultimate admission to Whitfield.

Roof Top Bridge

Several social workers and I liked to play bridge during our lunch break. My mother taught me the game when I was in high school, so I had basic knowledge of the game. My mother was a member of bridge clubs in Tupelo. While the ladies were playing bridge, they would go around the table and ask about their children. When they got to my mother, who had a very dry sense of humor, she said, "Bunny is in Whitfield," and didn't say that I worked there. "Oh, Virginia, we are so sorry. I hope he will be ok."

When the weather was nice, we social work bridge players climbed out a window in our office and set up a table and chairs on the roof of the administration building. No one knew that we were on the roof playing cards.

42+68+31+278=?

How fast can you add these numbers up in your head? How fast can you add them up with a handheld calculator or using paper and pencil? A middle-aged female patient living in one of the buildings in the back service could add these, or any numbers, faster than someone using a calculator. If I remember correctly, she was diagnosed as schizophrenic and would remain in the back service for continued care, which really meant there were no plans for her to ever be discharged. The physician responsible for this building told me about her. Another social worker and I came up with a short math quiz that the social worker would calculate on paper, and I would add on the calculator. She was given the quiz, and before the lead hit the paper, she gave the correct answer. She also beat my time using the calculator. She was an idiot savant--a person who is particularly skilled in one area, such as math or music. She did not function very well in real-life situations, but she could amaze people with her math skills. The answer is 419.

The Hog Pen

A middle-aged female patient with intellectual disabilities who had spent most of her life in the back service was very friendly and had a good relationship with everyone in her cottage. Whenever someone talked to her, she would show them her hands, which were missing some fingers. She said when she was a baby, she crawled into the family's hog pen and the hogs chewed some of her fingers off each hand. I can't imagine how terrifying that would have been for her. But she would always show me her hands whenever I made rounds in her building.

Muumuu's, But Not Hawaiian Style

Female patients who did not have personal clothes from home or money to buy clothes would wear a hospital-issued muumuu--a loose Hawaiian type of dress that would hang from the shoulders. These particular ones were not brightly colored but rather made from drab cotton material. It was often sad to see the women wearing them because they were one size fits most, and most did not fit well.

Newspapers for Sale

Harvey T., a patient on the back service, delivered the *Clarion-Ledger* for 40 years to patients and employees at Whitfield. In 1975, after 50 years of hospitalization, Harvey was released from the hospital and transferred to a boarding home in Jackson.

Harry O.

Harry O. was a long-term patient at Whitfield who was well known on the hospital grounds. He was easy to spot with his golfing pants, hat, and long socks. He was a golfer who was instrumental in developing Whitfield's 3-hole course. Harry was the groundsman and spent his days working on the golf course. I did not know him personally, but I knew him by reputation. According to Dr. Bill Parker, Harry often took the hospital bus into Jackson, where his wife lived. At one time, he lived in Building 21, which was the first building on the right going into the hospital. It was once for high-functioning patients who ran the building without direct supervision.[19]

Blow That Harmonica!

Austin, a White male in Building 82, was a short, stocky man who was quite talented at playing his harmonica. He could play any old-time song and was especially good at playing a song while barking like a hound dog chasing a coon or a train. He told me that he had been playing the harmonica since he was a boy, and it brought joy to his life. I asked if I could tape record his music if I didn't identify him. The next day, I took my portable tape recorder to his building, and he played a dozen songs. Patients and employees gathered around us in the yard; some clapped, and some danced. He played for so long that he started gasping for air, so I made him stop playing. I was afraid he would exhaust himself. I still have that cassette recording and will post his "concert" on my website: www.oldbluepublishing.com.

Charles Fortenberry "Do you know?"

Charles Fortenberry was a patient at Whitfield who spent most of his life institutionalized. From an early age he was diagnosed with childhood schizophrenia. Fortenberry was an avid reader of history, specifically military history. He did book reports for the *Grapevine* newspaper and was a reporter for his cottage in the back service. He was very bright and took immense pride in asking employees questions. He figured they would not know the answers. "Do you know that..." and if you could not answer, he would provide the answer and quickly walk away.

Although he did not make eye contact very often, he would talk about his family and his life at Whitfield. He knew interesting facts about many of the patients. Charles Fortenberry was discharged to a boarding home in Jackson and finally to his own apartment. He was seen in downtown Jackson often and continued his "Do you know…" with strangers on the street. After I left Whitfield, I worked downtown where I would run into him periodically. He would always begin, "Do you know?" He joined the downtown Galloway Methodist Church and attended Sunday School. My wife, who was in his Sunday School class, said he was interested in discussing Catholicism and the Pope with her when he found out she worked at St Dominic's Hospital.

When Charles (in his 70s) died of cardiac arrest in 2014, a memorial service was held at Galloway. His family and friends from church and Whitfield employees attended. His obituary read, "A man of many interests, possessed of encyclopedic knowledge, he loved meeting new friends and keeping in touch with family and old friends. He was an enthusiastic and eclectic baker, collector, correspondent, churchgoer, football fan, gift-giver, golfer, music lover, news-follower, raconteur, reader, traveler, and volunteer."[20]

Back Service Activities

The back service, or continued care service, was located towards the back of the hospital campus. It was comprised of cottages for patients who were not ready to be discharged and needed further treatment. In reality, many of these patients were living at Whitfield. It was their home. They had no discharge options. Many had been institutionalized at Whitfield for their entire adult lives. It was common for some patients to have lived at Whitfield for over thirty years. Many families did not want their relatives back home. And many long-time patients had no family.

The cottages for males were on one side of the campus, and those for females on the other end. The cottages were classified for distinct types of patients. There were buildings for disturbed patients, people with epilepsy, and long-term care patients. There was also an infirmary for patients who needed assistance with the activities of their daily living. While male and female back service buildings were on opposite ends of the campus from each other, that did not mean that patients could not get together. I took this photo in 1977 in front of one of the female cottages. Tommy visited Lois often at her cottage, and they were good friends. Lois is wearing one of the hospital- made dresses. Tommy is wearing the traditional hospital khaki pants and a shirt. Many of the older men wore hospital-issued brogans if they didn't personally own shoes.

Photo of Two Patients. Photo taken by author

The patient store was always a good meeting place for patients, but there were also the library and the church. The recreation and occupational therapy departments provided many activities for all the patients, including patients who were unable to have ground privileges. Dances were held in the auditorium, and patients could visit, dance, or just listen to music. The Jules Barlow Orchestra was one of the bands that played often from the early 1960s to the late 1970s.

The Grapevine reported in 1957 that for many of the dances, there would be as many as two hundred couples and several hundred more spectators from the hospital population.

There were always social activities on the campus. Looking back from the 1950s to the late 1970s, there was a wide variety of clubs for both men and women patients. These included the Literary Club, Glee Club, Current Events Club, History Club, Art Club, Garden Club, Book Review Club, Homemaker's Club, and Poetry Club. *The Grapevine* announced the times for the club meetings and then, in the next edition, announced those who attended.

The Recreation Department program evolved over the years, providing more activities for the patients. Sports included softball, basketball, volleyball, badminton, table tennis, and, of course, golf. An Easter Egg Hunt in 1977 had seven hundred participants looking for 4,600 boiled and dyed eggs. There were street dances, bingo games, watermelon-eating contests, trips to Jackson, train rides to Brookhaven, Jackson Mets baseball games, and field trips to Vicksburg Military Park. And, of course, shopping. Often, attendants from female cottages would take patients into Jackson or Pearl to shop. Social clubs from Metro Jackson would come to the hospital and arrange parties for the patients. In 1978, Cottage 36 had a charm school and style show.

Who discovered the Mississippi River?

A Black man living on the back service was not only a chronic schizophrenic, but he was also mute. He would sometimes respond to questions, but most of the time he just smiled and laughed. The physician responsible for his cottage was taking medical students on their psychiatric rotation. As they approached the patient, the physician described the patient's chronic condition to the students and said the patient was smarter than he appeared. He asked the patient, "Who discovered the Mississippi River?" and the patient responded, "De Soto." The medical students were astounded by his answer. While it was not ethical, the physician had been coaching the patient to give the correct answer by teaching him to say "de 'so' toe." So, whenever the physician had students on rounds with him, he would go through the scenario of asking the patient who discovered the Mississippi River, and the patient would look at his foot and say, "de 'so' toe."

Three in a Canoe

I have always enjoyed the outdoors, especially hunting, fishing, hiking, and canoeing. Paddling a canoe was one of my favorite activities when I was younger. I had canoed down the Pearl River several times in a three-man raft and a few times in canoes. The Pearl River meanders from Neshoba County, Mississippi, for 444 miles, reaching the Gulf of Mexico. There were two memorable trips with two psychologists from the Psychology Department at Whitfield.

We canoed down the Pearl River starting at Jackson and camped on one of the many beautiful sand bars. We carried tents, food, a radio, and plenty of beer, necessary items for an overnight canoe trip only a few miles from Jackson. The other trip was down the Strong River near the D'Lo Water Park in D'Lo, Mississippi. Although the river was calm and slow-moving, we still had to paddle to keep ourselves centered and away from overhanging trees. This canoe trip was in the fall, and the temperature dropped at night, but we had the necessary beverages to keep going. We came off the river about dark and found a place to camp, set up our tents, built a fire, and ate supper. One of the better canoe trips. Of course, there is a lot more to this story.

Bo Bowen on the Strong River. Note the long hair and moustache.

I described these canoe trips to the physician I was working with, and he was very interested in our river exploits. He suggested a few more rivers across the state that we should canoe. He also suggested that we could map those rivers for camping and canoeing sites. Trading posts could be set up on those sites to provide guide services, from which people could rent canoes. We listened attentively and knew that the ideas the physician was coming up with were a bit over the top. When he excitedly suggested we would need a helicopter for emergencies on the rivers, we knew he needed some help, and we needed to avoid any more canoe talk with him. However, I was still working with him in the back service. His ideas made for interesting conversations with patients and staff. I did not have to report the physician to the chief of staff since the medical staff was aware of his behavior. I do not know if he was placed on leave of absence or if his employment was terminated, but he did not return to the hospital while I was working there.

Mr. Arthur

Mr. Arthur was a small, wiry, geriatric patient on the back service. I don't know how long he had lived at Whitfield, but it had been for a very long time. Whenever I made rounds in his building, I would ask him how he was doing, and he would always say, "Arthur is all right, but Ritis still hurts." (Arthritis)

What's Growing in the Greenhouse?

Just a rumor? I used to walk by the greenhouse which was down the street from the student nursing dormitory. The greenhouse at that time was covered in vines and bushes. The rumor was that it was closed temporarily because patients or employees were growing marijuana. I have no idea if this was true, but I do remember seeing it covered in vines and appearing vacant.

Who's Selling the Booze?

There were rumors from the administration that someone was selling liquor to patients and employees at the hospital. Patients were discovered intoxicated but would not tell who they bought the alcohol from or where they got it. It was like that scene from the Andy Griffith show in which Otis Campbell would not tell Andy where he was buying the moonshine whiskey. The staff targeted the patient store as the location for the illicit sale of alcohol. Patients would go to that store for food, coffee, and opportunities to socialize with other patients. It was decided that the only way to uncover the mystery was for someone to dress as a patient and "infiltrate" the store to find the culprits. I was chosen as the "patient" and was provided khaki pants, a work shirt, and a cap from the Volunteer Services clothes room so that I could walk around and mingle with the patients and keep my nose in the air for the smell of liquor. I probably never looked like a patient, but for about half a day, I asked questions and looked for intoxicated patients and employees. Although I was qualified to detect the smell of alcohol, I never found the source of the booze.

Fred Chaney, a well-known patient at the hospital, was called "The King of Whitfield" for his exploits in the 1940s-1950s--smuggling letters out of the hospital discussing the conditions, food, medical care, and patient abuse. Fred had a patient friend who had ground privileges and could ride the hospital bus into Jackson for the day. He lost those privileges when his doctor discovered that he was bringing Fred Chaney six packs of beer he bought in Jackson.

Jeremiah was a Bull Frog

I was working with Dr. Mary Hogan in Female Receiving, and another male social worker was working with Dr. Walterine Bell. A patient who had been admitted with a drug problem and was high as a kite was locked in a security cell that had a steel-screened door. Around that time, Valium was the drug of choice for many of the women admitted with drug problems. In the physician's office, we could hear the patient singing loudly the Three Dog Night song, "Joy to the World." She was singing *"Jeremiah was a bullfrog. Was a good friend of mine. I never understood a single word he said, but I helped him a-drink his wine. And he always had some mighty fine wine. Singin' joy to the world...*" Drs. Hogan and Bell explicitly told us NOT to go down the hall and check her out. That temptation was overwhelming since the patient was singing all the verses of the song.

We had to see her. We went to her cell and saw her sitting in the middle of the floor naked as a jaybird, singing as loudly as she could, "*Jeremiah was a bullfrog...*" We got our eyes full as she was an attractive woman. To this day, whenever I hear that song, I think about that patient and Dr. Hogan's disapproving eyes. I had a chance to hear Three Dog Night on the Gulf Coast on July 27, 2024, and that was their closing song. I knew all the words.

Kit Whitsett Fields, Artist

Kit was a cute, perky social worker who worked at Whitfield in the mid-to-late 1970s. She was a joy to be around--funny, and sometimes a little naïve when it came to understanding some of our jokes and stories. She worked hard and was well-liked by the social workers, administration, doctors, and patients. Kit had a talent for what she called just some "sketchings." Those sketches were quickly drawn on whatever piece of paper she had within reach. If it were time to take off a "month" sheet on the desk calendar, she would tear off a piece and draw on the back of it. My office was across from hers in the social work department, so I would sometimes see her at her desk "sketching." And if I were in her office when she finished a "drawing" and tossed it in the garbage, I would quickly retrieve it and have her autograph it. To me, her art was a treasure that I would always keep. I have several of her early Whitfield drawings framed in my office at home. She began painting professionally in 1995 and has won multiple local and regional awards over the years, including from the Southern Watercolor Society, the Mississippi Grand National Exhibition, and the Mississippi Watercolor Society. She was also chosen as the 2018 U.S.A. International Ballet Competition official artist.

Kit Fields, 1970's Whitfield sketch. Author's Personal property.

Haldol: A New Drug, Not Just for Patients

Haldol was approved by the FDA in 1967 and later introduced in the U.S. It was an antipsychotic medication used to treat schizophrenia and other psychoses. The new drug came both in concentrate and tablet form and was being introduced on Female Receiving. Dr. Mary Hogan wanted us social workers to understand the administration of the drug and had us hold out our finger while she used the eyedropper in the bottle to squeeze a drop on our finger. She asked all of us to taste the drop, which was bitter. She then poured each of us a medicine cup of orange juice and placed one drop in each container. We drank a cup of orange juice and could not taste the Haldol. And that was the point. Patients being prescribed Haldol were given the medicine in a cup of orange juice.

Can I Have Your "Short"?

Smoking was allowed everywhere at Whitfield. Anyone who smoked cigarettes was popular and sought after on the campus. Patients who had their own money could buy cigarettes at the patient store. Or their families would supply them with plenty of cigarettes to last them until the next visit. Patients who did not have much money to buy their own cigarettes would often buy one cigarette at a time from other patients. When I smoked at Whitfield, there were patients who would ask for my "short." A short could be a half-smoked cigarette, or one burned almost to the filter. There were patients who would ask for your "short" just as soon as you lit it up. Cigarettes dropped or crushed out on the ground or on sidewalks would be picked up and relit. I was an easy mark since I usually gave the patients my "short" or one right out of the cigarette pack. The only other alternative for patients with no money was the free hospital tobacco called "Our Advertiser." Patients would be given a sack of loose tobacco and rolling papers so they could roll their own cigarettes.

Only those with experience could roll a cigarette without the tobacco falling out. Often, we saw patients light up their rolled cigarettes that would go up in flames in their face if they were not rolled correctly. I tried to roll the Whitfield tobacco with the supplied papers to see the effort it required. The tobacco was very leafy and did not have a good odor, and the papers did not hold up well. I could clearly see the skill needed. I went to Brown-Williamson Tobacco in Jackson and asked them to donate their Bugler cigarette roller machines and rolling papers. The next day I gave the machines to my back service buildings and taught the employees how to use the machines. They were successful and rolled cigarettes for the patients.

MISSISSIPPI STATE HOSPITAL

W. L. Jaquith, M.D.
Chief of Medical Staff

WHITFIELD, MISS.

James C. Stubbs
Director

Memo

To: Mr. Sidney Tatum, Business Manager

From: Ernest Bowen, Social Worker EB

Re: Cigarette Rolling Machines, tobacco, etc.

On 4/4/77 I called the Corr-Williams Tobacco Co., 442 N. Mill, Jackson, Telephone 353-5871. A case of Bugler Cigarette Rolling Machines (12 to a case) is $19.20 or $1.60 each. The kit includes the machine, two sacks of bugler tobacco, cigarette carrying case, and two packages of gummed cigarette papers (100 papers per pack).

A case of Bugler tobacco is $36.36. If my calculations are correct that should be around 25¢ a sack X 144 for a case. I believe the size of the bugler tobacco is at least twice as large as the Our Advertiser which we use here at the hospital. I have been told and I have also smoked both brands and the Bugler rolls better and is not as bitter as the other brand. Actually I wouldn't smoke either if I had my choice.

A case of Top gummed cigarette papers, 20 packages to a case is $46.20. The person I talked with did not know how many papers were to a package but for that price I am assuming it to be a large amount.

Female Recieving and Building #23 are both using the machines and so far I have heard no complaints, just that they are running out of the gummed papers. I have been buying them locally for 12¢ a pack which is no burden but if the hospital decides to use the above I'm sure we'll get our money's worth.

Letter to Sidney Tatum, personal copy

MISSISSIPPI STATE HOSPITAL

W. L. Jaquith, M.D.
Chief of Medical Staff

WHITFIELD, MISS.

James C. Stubbs
Director

August 5,1977

Memo

To: Mr. Sidney Tatum
Business Manager

From: Ernest Bowen
Social Worker

On 5/26/77 I supplied Building #23 with three Bugler cigarette rolling machines, one box of gummed papers, and eight boxes of tobacco. This was an experimental project to see if using cigarette rolling machines would be beneficial and practical. The eight boxes of tobacco that was furnished was a measured amount which was equal to the amount supplied to Building #23 by the hospital. The Our Advertiser tobacco, which is supplied by the hospital is usually dry and stale but it is more convenient for patients to carrty with them. The Bugler tobacco is almost twice the amount and size of the hospital tobacco, but I feel that it would be impractical for a patient to carry this much tobacco at one time. I have smoked both tobaccos and even though the Bugler tobacco is not as harsh, both are equally bad. The three cigarette machines that I provided for Building #23 are still in use and are still in good shape. The actual "life" of these machines is unknown. The gummed cigarette papers, which are essential for the working of the cigarette rolling machines, can be easily wasted if they are not used properly. Out of the twenty four books of gummed papers supplied to the building, fifteen books have been used.

I feel this experiment has shown that the cigarette rolling machines can be put to good use here at the hospital and when used properly, could be economical. The floors on Building #23 seem cleaner and this could be attributed to the machines. When a patient rolls their own cigarette by hand, most of the tobacco falls to the floor. I have also noted that the burn factor between a machine rolled cigarette, and a hand rolled cigarette is higher for the hand rolled cigarette. For some unknown reason the machine rolled cigarette burns slower and is less apt to "blow up" from the initial lighting of the cigarette.

Mrs. Donna Davidson and Mrs. Linda Harrison, R.N.'s on the Male Continued Care Service were supplied with the cigarette rolling machines and papers and this presently leaves me with two machines.

If I can furnish you with additional information, please let me know.

Letter to Sidney Tatum

"Smoke, Smoke, Smoke that Cigarette"

Toye G., a long-time patient at Whitfield, would walk around to the back of the administration building, stop, place his hands on his hips, lean back, and sing loudly:

Smoke, smoke, smoke that cigarette,

Puff, puff, puff and if you smoke yourself to death.

Tell St Peter at the Golden Gate that you hate to make him wait.

But you just gotta have another cigarette.

(Words by Merle Travis and Tex Williams, 1947)

Prince Albert in a Can

A can of Prince Albert tobacco and tobacco papers could be bought at the patient store. It was good tobacco and smelled good when smoked in either a pipe or rolled into a cigarette. I didn't roll the tobacco in a cigarette, but I occasionally smoked it in one of the pipes that I had inherited from my grandfather.

A can of Prince Albert had one more beneficial use when it was empty. Patients would boil coffee in the can. They would punch holes on each end of the flip top, run pieces of wire through the holes, and then run the two wires into an electrical outlet in their rooms. The electricity was enough to boil the water to make coffee. It was also extremely dangerous, and the patient would often get a good shock connecting or disconnecting the wires from the outlet. When we made patient rounds, we would look around the beds and outlets and often discover the "coffee pots." I don't remember seeing these Prince Albert cans in the female cottages, but I bet they were there.

Rev. Ike and His Prayer Cloths

It was common to find reading material and prayer cloths in the female cottages from Rev. Ike, who said, "The Bible says that Jesus rode on a borrowed ass. But I would rather ride in a Rolls

Royce than ride somebody's ass!" Better known as Dr. Frederick Eikerenkoetter, he will arrive in Los Angeles tomorrow "riding in a pink, rose-covered Rolls Royce." (*Action!* Vol. 8, No. 74, August 1974.0)

The Church Steps In

Mrs. Karl Stauss was the secretary for the Methodist Conference, and she and her daughters were personal friends of mine. She was the daughter of Dr. Henry Boswell, long-time superintendent of the Mississippi State TB Sanatorium, later to be named the Boswell Regional Center. I told her that many of the Whitfield buildings needed some sprucing up and asked if she would get the word out to the women's circles around the state. Mrs. Stauss sent out a request through the *Methodist Advocate* newsletter asking for donations to the hospital. The notice went out to all the Methodist Churches in the conference and asked people to contact Ms. Guice or me with donations. We received such donations as televisions, coffee urns, magazines, and money from Sunday School classes. A check for $30.24 was sent to cover the cost of curtain rods in a female cottage. We received some used television sets from Natchez with a request for us to have them repaired if needed and send the bill to the Sunday School Class. Each donation was acknowledged by a thank-you note for the donor's support to Whitfield patients.

Free the Whitfield 2500 T-shirt property of Bo Bowen

Free The Whitfield 2500

For many years the ACLU fought in court against involuntary commitments, against the housing of non-dangerous patients without cause, and for the right to treatment. The *O'Connor v. Donaldson* case, which defined the rights of mentally ill people, was the first to reach the Supreme Court. It also helped pave the way for the deinstitutionalization of thousands of mentally ill patients across the country in the 1970s. Mississippi State Hospital was not immune to the ruling and knew that deinstitutionalization would be another priority issue for staff.

It was not long before David Seth Michaels, an attorney with the Mississippi Mental Health Project and Community Legal Services, said the ruling was clear, and patients at Whitfield had a right to treatment. He said it was unconstitutional for the hospital to confine patients against their will if they were not dangerous to themselves or others. Michaels said social workers should "work overtime" to find places for those people. He estimated two-thirds of the 3,000 Whitfield patients could live elsewhere.

In his celebration of the Supreme Court ruling and the green light to deinstitutionalize Whitfield, Michaels created and sold T-shirts that said "Free the Whitfield 2500 Mississippi Mental Health Project" on the back, and a depiction of a Thorazine SKF T69 capsule on the front. It was not long before SKF (Smith Kline & French), the manufacturer of Thorazine, let him know that it was a copyright infringement and to cease producing and selling the T-shirts. However, Michaels wrote back to SKF and said it was produced based on the First Amendment. They didn't reply, and he continued selling the T-shirts. The first series of T-shirts said, "Free the Whitfield 3000."

Claire Crawford

Claire was the Reimbursement Clerk in the administration building and worked with families to pay for their patients' hospital services. I always thought she was naive, but she was a sweet young lady who did not approve of deer hunting. A friend I worked with, Dr. Neil Murphree, and I hunted together. We decided to present her with a special deer trophy. We kept the buck's scrotum, dried it, and wrapped it in a box with ribbons and presented it to her. She was not too impressed and gave it back to us. I guess it was the thought that counted, right?

Whitfield Autopsies

Autopsies were sometimes performed at the hospital morgue located in the basement of Male Receiving. It was a dark, cold, damp, forbidding place with two large doors wide enough for an ambulance to back in, park, and unload the deceased patient. A forensic pathologist from Jackson, Mississippi, conducted the autopsies. A University of Mississippi medical student/ friend of mine on psychiatric rotation at Whitfield asked me if I wanted to see an autopsy. With much hesitation, I agreed. We entered through the two wide doors and met the pathologist. He made it clear that if we wanted to watch the autopsy, we must stay through the entire procedure. If we got sick or nauseated, we could not leave. We agreed, and he had us pull a large, Black man from the cooler and lay him out on the table. A large light shone down on him. The light was strong enough so that all of us could clearly see each cut that the pathologist made and its results. Above the deceased man was a microphone hanging from a wire so the pathologist could document the autopsy.

He opened the patient's chest and showed us his lungs, which were black as soot. He said that the patient was obviously a heavy smoker, which got my attention since I smoked at the time. Each organ he removed from the deceased man was examined and placed on the table. By the time the pathologist got to crack open his skull, I was about to lose it. All I could do was hold my breath and close my eyes. I cut back on my cigarette smoking that day.

The Disaster Drill

On November 3, 1977, the hospital took part in a disaster drill. The scenario was a plane that left the nearby airport and crashed into Building 29 on the grounds of the hospital. Staff employees were to have distinct roles to play. There would be staff who were injured from the plane crash, and the nursing staff would triage and take care of the wounded passengers. I remember I was one of the passengers. I had on makeup to show I had a head injury and a broken arm. Each hospital department had a written disaster plan.

Gail Burns, Night Supervisor

Gail Burns was a night supervisor on Male Receiving and was well-liked by all staff. I got to know him by seeing him often at Male Receiving and on the grounds of the hospital. He was a kind man, helpful to employees and patients. He always wore his white attendant uniform clean and starched. On Saturday night, May 1, 1976, a family dropped off one of its members around 10:30 p.m. to be admitted. The hospital policy at the time was for night admissions to be escorted by a security guard to Male Receiving, where they would be admitted and changed into hospital clothes. Within one hour of admission, the patient had stabbed Gail to death with a butcher knife. The patient also stabbed a security guard several times, who was left in critical condition. The patient escaped but was captured the next morning, charged with capital murder and attempted murder. (Clarion-*Ledger*, May 3, 1976.)

I remember hearing the news of Gail's death on Monday and was stunned to know I would never get to talk with him again. His death was the first of an employee I knew while I worked at the hospital.

The murder of Gail Burns left everyone on edge and more cautious around patients. Word of patients assaulting attendants, nurses, social workers, and doctors was well known at Whitfield. No one was immune to these attacks when dealing with disturbed patients. I had unfortunately learned from my attendant days to be aware of my surroundings and not to turn my back on a disturbed patient. A mental health group sent a telegram to then-Governor Cliff Finch asking for an investigation of Whitfield's safety conditions.

Self Defense Course

The personnel department sponsored a self-defense course for employees after Gail Burns' stabbing death. All employees needed to know how to protect themselves in the buildings and on the grounds of the hospital. We were instructed on how to break out of a hold, how to disarm a patient who had a knife or other weapon, and how to physically restrain a patient. Participants were paired with another employee, and we were trained in self-defense tactics in the green space behind the administration building. My partner was Preston Piazza who was employed with the Personnel Department. Because he was a big burly guy, trying to throw him over my shoulder and restrain him was a feat. He tossed me around like a wet noodle. Below are the instructions for using the "Rear Windmill Defense." I seriously doubt I could have thought to use this defense tactic when I was attacked by the patient in Hydro Ward.

(3) REAR WINDMILL DEFENSE. If an opponent grasps your throat from the rear execute the following defense: Make a fist with your right hand, lock your right arm at the elbow and extend your right fist skyward bringing the right bicep as close to your right ear as possible. Pivot on the balls of your feet to the right rotating the upper part of the body to the right. In a looping motion, to the rear and to your opponent's left, encircle your opponent's arms by driving your right arm down and over your opponent's arms breaking the hold. Bring your right fist up to your cheek locking your opponent's arms, above the elbow, under your right armpit. Extend and join the fingers of the left hand and raise it to shoulder level. Drive the knife edge of your left hand into your opponent's kidney area.

Defensive Tactics. Property of Bo Bowen

The Rankin County Deputies

A patient from Rankin County was brought to the hospital for admission by the Rankin County Deputy Sheriffs. During the admission process, the patient escaped and raced upstairs to our

Social Service offices. There was a lot of screaming because the patient had a knife and was wildly thrashing it around when we got to him. Two deputies, another social worker, and I tried to restrain the man. We charged him with a chair, pinning him up against the wall to keep him from stabbing us. That's when the deputy, who was quite excited by this time, pulled out his mace pen to immobilize the patient. The problem was that he was not pointing it at the patient, but instead was pointing it at us! He sprayed us for what seemed like an eternity until he took his finger off the button. We were almost immobilized from the mace, but we kept pushing the chair against the patient and were able to take the knife out of his hand. Hospital security arrived by the time we had him restrained. I suppose we should have restrained the deputy. I was sent home to wash up, change clothes, and return to work. That was the first and last time I have ever been sprayed with mace.

Dr. James Starry, Big Band Fan

Dr. James Starry was director of the Psychology Department at Whitfield. Because I would sometimes bring patients over for testing, we eventually struck up a friendship. We were both interested in big band music and jazz, and often talked about bands we liked. He had a stereo in his office from which he would play a cut or two from an LP. I remember we got tickets to hear the Stan Kenton Orchestra at Clinton High School, and he picked me up in his Avanti sports car. Another time when Ahmad Jamal was playing at a Black juke joint on Highway 49, we wanted to hear him. We went in and were surprised to see that we were the only White people in the bar. However, we were welcomed with beer and sat with some strangers to enjoy the music. Maybe we were accepted because we wanted to listen to the performer. Jamal played his famous rendition of "Poinciana."

Memo to Social Service Staff About Work Habits

The first memo on conduct was certainly directed at me since I was prone to doing these "things." It was no secret I was the one acting up. But to be clear – I got my work done every day, made my rounds with the doctors, and made my own rounds to see patients after the doctors' rounds. Even though I was experienced in breaking Mr. Ward's rules, he recognized me as someone who had the experience needed to be a member of the policy committee to study patient monies.

L. Jaquith, M.D.
of Medical Staff

WHITFIELD, MISS.

James C. Stubbs
Director

March 10, 1976

MEMO

TO: Social Work And Secretarial Staff

FROM: Doyce B. WArd, ACSW
Director, Social Work Department

SUBJECT: Personal Office Conduct, Use of Time, Etc.

It is felt that with a group as large as we have that some general rules or guidelines for office conduct and for use of our time is indicated. Below are some guidelines that I am asking that we abide by and which I think will help us to establish a better work atmosph ere.

1. Please refrain from sitting on any of the desks and from propping your foot up on any of the desks. Sitting on your own or someone else's desk is unnessary and as you all know we have ample chairs for everyone.

2. Please refrain from engaging in Prolonged Conversation in the secretarial area or in the hall about matters unrelated to our work. Such conversation can interfere with the work of others and especially the secretaries. If you need to confer with another worker about a patient on some other matter related to work please go to the worker's office or your own office.

3. Please let me know if on a regular basis you have periods of time during which you have nothing to do. I would also like to know if you feel you are overloaded with work and feel the need of some adjustment in your work load.

4. Please refrain from any sort of playful activity or horse play or whatever it is called. This sort of activity is uncalled for, is unprofessional, and is in no way conducive to the proper work atmosphere.

5. If for any reason you are unavoidably delayed and are unable to get back from your lunch hour at the proper time please call in to Mrs. Lee. There may be a family member or someone else waiting for you and Mrs. Lee needs to know if you are going to be delayed.

If any of you have any questions about the above rules please talk to me. I am hoping that we can get by with as few rules as possible but if any of you have further suggestions about what you think we need to do please let me know. Your co-operation in this endeavor will be appreciated.

DBW:el

Letter from Ward - Personal Copy

MISSISSIPPI STATE HOSPITAL

W. L. Jaquith, M.D.
Chief of Medical Staff

WHITFIELD, MISS.

James C. Stubbs
Director

February 2, 1976

To: Mr. James Stubbs

From: Doyce B. Ward

Subject: Policy committee regarding patients funds.

I have designated Mr. Ernest Bowen as the representative from the Social Work Department to serve on the committee that will review the matter of patient monies and make recommendations regarding policies. When Mr. Bowen was a college student he worked at the hospital as an attendant and he has had some experience that could be helpful to the committee.

DBW
Doyce B. Ward, ACSW
Director, Social Work Department

cc: Mr. Ernest Bowen
Mr. Harold Rimmer
Miss Bettie Lee
Mr. Dave Gayden

ds

Patient Monies Committee. Personal Copy

MISSISSIPPI STATE HOSPITAL

W. L. Jaquith, M.D.
Chief of Medical Staff

WHITFIELD, MISS.
March 30, 1976

James C. Stubbs
Director

To: Mr. Doyce B. Ward, ACSW, Director
Social Work Department

From: Ernest Bowen
Finance Committee

Re: Patient's Monies

1. Hospital Supervisors are responsible for the routine withdrawals of funds from the resident's account and for the resident's personal use. If a resident runs out of funds he should see the supervisor for his building.

   Social Workers should not withdraw money for residents except in emergencies, when being discharged, or for shopping. Your copy of the withdrawal slip should be sent to the Medical Records Department on an appropriate form stating the purpose of the withdrawal.

2. Social Workers should be aware of residents with excess or idle funds in the Accounting Department. The Cashier, Supervisor or charge attendant should be able to give you this information.

3. When a resident is discharged the Social Worker should check the Accounting Office and ward to see that the resident receives his money.

4. On weekends Social Workers are responsible for receiving money or checks for resident's medical or personal expenses. A receipt must always be given to anyone leaving money. Money for a new admission should have date of admission, County of admission, and correspondent's name and address on the receipt for the Cashier. The money collected on the weekends should be placed in a safe place until Monday Morning.

5. The Finance Committee has recommended that each resident who is working for the hospital be assigned a Social Worker to counsel with him or her on the handling of their paycheck. There are 41 resident-employees at Mississippi State Hospital earning an average income of $160.00 a month. These residents receive no counseling in spending and managing their money. Out of these 41,

only 5 residents leave most of their checks for deposit in the accounting office. The remainder cash their checks and keep the money on them. One resident was recently found to have over $1800 in cash on him and he very reluctantly had it deposited into an account for him. Some of the residents have reported money taken from them after cashing their checks and many were reported to have gambled or given their money away. We cannot control how a resident uses his money but we can counsel with them in how to manage their money and show them how their money can be spent or saved. This does not apply only to residents employees but to any resident carrying large sums of money on them.

Any comments or suggestions would be appreciated.

Ernest Bowen

Ernest Bowen
Finance Committee

EB/hm

The Nurse Had Her Sail Up

Patsy R. worked with Dr. Robert Ritter and often on her lunch breaks or after work would launch her small sailboat and sail around Whitfield Lake. It is a beautiful lake with ducks and geese landing in the water and strutting along the banks. It was always a treat to watch her sail slowly across the lake because it was so relaxing.

Mental Health Centers

Dr. William Jaquith, former director of Mississippi State Hospital, pushed for mental health centers in the 1950s, and for that very reason, the following memo was written. And still, there are issues with mental health centers and the services they provide in their communities for the mentally ill.

MSH - 14

Mississippi State Hospital

WHITFIELD, MISSISSIPPI

CASE NOTES

Case No.____________

Year No.____________ Name______________________

5/13/76

MEMO

TO: MR. DOYCE B. WARD, ACSW
DIRECTOR, SOCIAL SERVICE DEPARTMENT

FROM: ERNEST BOWEN, SOCIAL WORKER, SOCIAL SERVICE DEPARTMENT

Re: Mental Health Centers

This is to confirm our discussion a couple of weeks ago about the location of the Satellite Mental Health Centers. Regions V, and XI have given us a comprehensive breakdown of the Counties they serve and the location of their offices in each County. When I refer a patient to a Regional Mental Health Center I give the m the location of the Administrative Offices and tell them that the Center will be in touch with them shortly after their discharge from the hospital. On numerous occasions patients have stated that their home, example Smith County, is too far to travel to receive help in Meridian. At this point I question that the patient will ever receive follow-up care. If there is a Mental Health Center in Smith County, I am unaware of it. This example applies to most of the Regional Centers.

I request that we notify all the Regional Mental Health Centers by letter or proper form and request from them a listing of all their Satellite Offices and if possible their directors and office hours. I also feel it would be beneficial for us to know how each center contacts our referrals and the time involved.

I feel if we had this information we would be more knowledgeable in talking with our patients about referral and making sure that they receive the best possible after-care treatment.

Ernest Bowen, Social Worker

EB/hm

MISSISSIPPI STATE HOSPITAL

W. L. Jaquith, M.D.
Chief of Medical Staff

WHITFIELD, MISS.
June 27, 1977

James C. Stubbs
Director

M E M O

TO: MRS MAE ROBERTS, MS. EVELYN AYERS, MRS. GAYE BECK, MS. SMITH AND MRS. LYONS.

FROM: DOYCE B. WARD, ACSW, DIRECTOR SOCIAL WORK DEPARTMENT

Thank you for taking your time to meet with us on 6/24/77 to discuss some of our concerns relative to the procedures used to process patient's mail. It turned out the problem was not as great as I had thought. Nevertheless from our meeting if I remember correctly the following things were clarified:

1. The hospital in past years used to furnish stamps for patients but it does not do so now. There had been some misunderstanding regarding this up until recently.

2. One of the primary problems for the Social Workers in past years relative to the patient's mail has been inadequate or bizarre addresses and or the absence of the patient's name on the out side of the envelope. This of course made it difficult for the Social Worker to know who wrote the letter if for any reason the letter was not mailable. It was discussed and thought to be desirable for attendant personnel to make an effort to see that the patient's name hereafter was on the envelope before it was left for mailing.

3. It was decided that in the event a patient did not have a stamp he should be instructed by the attendant and or the nurse to ask his Social Worker about a stamp. Thereafter it would be the Social Worker's responsibility to help the patient get a stamp and to talk to the patient about what he should do thereafter regarding stamps.

DBW/hm

Mr. Ward Memo. Personal Copy

Patient Mail

I have learned that the Social Services Department currently tries to provide patients with stamps, so this procedure has not changed.

Example of an unreadable envelope from a patient in Cottage S. The envelope and the letter enclosed could not be read; therefore, it was to be tossed. However, it intrigued me, so I kept the envelope.

Patient Letter. Personal Copy

Throwing in the Towel

I sent this memo to Mr. Ward saying that I was admitting defeat with my ideas that I thought could make positive changes at the hospital. Most of the time, my memos and questions were either ignored or I was told, "We will get back to you." The hospital administration and even some patient-building employees could not see the advances we could make if we could be working together from the same page. The culture of the hospital has been shown to be stagnant in advancing changes or in thinking outside of the box. The memo was not sent as a warning.

MISSISSIPPI STATE HOSPITAL

DR. W. L. JAQUITH, *Director*

WHITFIELD, MISS.

November 17, 1976

To: Mr. Doyce Ward, Director
Social Work Department

From: Ernest Bowen
Social Worker

As of this date I have decided that I will no longer become involved in or try to bring about change in Mississippi State Hospital. Any ideas or suggestions that I may have in the future will be kept to myself. I have felt very strongly about this hospital since I was an attendant and I have always wanted to see procedures and hospital routines run smoothly not only for the patients but for the other employees. I have stuck my neck out on numerous occasions to speak out on changes that not only I wanted but others wanted. I suppose I have finally seen the realism that I have been involved in and realize that in this hospital it is best to remain silent and let *Memo to Mr. Ward. Personal Copy*

Memo to Mr. Ward, Personal Copy

Patients' Finance Committee

MISSISSIPPI STATE HOSPITAL

W. L. Jaquith, M.D.
Chief of Medical Staff

WHITFIELD, MISS.

James C. Stubbs
Director

December 12, 1977

Mr. James Stubbs, Director
Miss. State Hospital
Whitfield, Miss.

Dear Mr. Stubbs,

The Patient's Finance Committee would like to see the Hospital provide a desirable place for patients, employees, visitors and families to visit and this place to be operated by the Hospital. Please see recommendations below.

I. Build a new store at a central location on hospital grounds

II. Guidelines for operating present store.

A. Maintain premises according to Chief Burnaham - See Attachment.

B. Price list posted on all goods sold. This price list should reflect surrounding area prices.

C. Discontinue practice of cashing check and money orders for patients.

D. Not to employ patient help without prior approval by Vocational Rehabilitation.

E. Remove juke box from patient store.

After you have reviewed the above recommendations by the Finance Committee, we will be open for further discussion at your convenience.

Sincerely,

Dave P. Gayden
Chairman

Ernest L. Bowen
Committee Member

Bettie Lee
Committee Member

Harold Rimmer
Committee Member

DPG/bl

Memo to Mr. Stubbs

PAGE 1

MISSISSIPPI STATE HOSPITAL

W. L. Jaquith, M.D.
Chief of Medical Staff

WHITFIELD, MISS.
August 24, 1978

James C. Stubbs
Director

TO: Mr. Sidney Tatum, Chairman
Inventory Supply/Property Control Subcommittee

FROM: Ernest Bowen

As of September 1, 1978, I will no longer be employed at Mississippi State Hospital and therefore unable to continue membership in this Subcommittee. I had hoped that this committee would be able to meet again after the initial organizational meeting of 3/16/78. At that time the members were asked to think of problem areas, in the hospital with short range solutions and to identify kinds of information needed to perform taksk efficiently. We were to present our ideas at the next committee meeting for discussion and possible action. I therefore, submit the following suggestions:

1. Printed material and office supplies commonly run out and there is usually a long delay in printing and purchasing. A system could be developed to keep an adequate level of stock on hand at all times.

2. Heating and Cooling Systems- A system could be developed to cut the steam heat off during cool days and nights when it is not needed; it usually takes as long as two days before the system can be cut off and as long as two days before it can be cut back on. Most offices end up using electric heaters during this time and this has caused electrical problems, especially in the Social Work Department. When the heat is not cut off during the warmer days, air conditioning systems are usually running. This is a waste of energy and this should be a priority.

3. It would be safe to state that the majority of all outside building lights burn 24 hours a day. I have taken it upon myself to cut off the outside lights of the Administration Building most every morning for the last four months. According to average figures, if I did not cut off two of the three lights, it would cost the hospital $10.50 a month. Considering the number of lights left on throughout the hospital, the figures would be astronomical. I suggest that the hospital try and conserve energy and use the money that is saved for services that could be used in the hospital.

4. It is my understanding that in the future, the hospital will have a museum on the grounds and that the Hydro-Therapy equipment in the basement of Building #23 will be housed in that museum. Some of the equipment has been vandalized and the basement is continuing to deteriorate. I have made numerous attempts to have the equipment salvaged over the last three years with no success. I would suggest that steps be taken to salvage the equipment now and not wait another three years.

5. The sign in and sign out post for some of the Female Continued Care Service employees is on Building #23. There are parking problems, traffic congestion and because of this there have been several automobile accidents. A suggestion would be to have several posts located throughout the hospital to relieve the congestion in hopes of avoiding future accidents.

6. There is presently a shortage of men's clothing in the Volunteer Service Department due to Male receiving patients' ability to get more clothes than they actually need. It is reported that patients from Male Receiving have sold the clothes they get to other patients. Volunteer Service employees have been threatened by these patients on numerous occasions when they did not get all the clothes they wanted. I suggest that no clothes be given to Male Receiving patients unless their Social Worker feels that there is a need. The mens' clothes should be used exclusively for Male Continued Care patients who may require long term care and have no other resources. The deteriorating condition and lack of space in the Volunteer Service Department has been overlookd in the past and since it is one of the most useful services in the hospital, one would think their facility could be up-graded.

7. The urinal in the men's restroom in the Social Work Department has been inoperable for over six years. This creates a health problem not only for employees, but patients and visitors who come to our office. Attempts have been made in the past to correct this situation with no results. I suggest that a plumber inspect the fixture and make any necessary repairs.

8. On 8/24/78, Male Receiving employees brought to the Social Work Department 70 separate items that were left on Male Receiving when the patients were discharged. It will be the responsibility of our department to get the patient's mailing address, wrap the package, send a cover letter and mail the package. The cost of these 70 articles will cost approximately $40.00 for postage. This is also costly and time consuming to our staff. Male Receiving usually brings these "forgotten" items on the average of every three to four months. A system needs to be developed to see that each patient receives their belongings at the time of their discharge.

9. Personnel problems, Low Morale, No incentives, Poor communication between departments. I have found, as many others have, that at this time the morale of this hospital is at its lowest ever. Employees have very little input in hospital policies and many are never given the opportunity to express their feeling without some form of reprisal. I would propose that:

(a) A suggestion box, with printed forms for all employees, be

(a) cont.
located at the Information Desk in the Administration Building to give employees an opportunity to voice their opinions.

(b) Develop a General Staff for Department Heads, Supervisors, key personnel and representatives for the Psychiatric Aides, to discuss problem areas with possible solutions and to meet with the Medical Staff periodically to work on any problems that may exist. This could help alleviate any communication problems between departments.

(c) Employees be aware of any openings in any department that they could qualify and meet the requirements. The Merit System furnishes to the Personnel Department information on available jobs that exist in this hospital and this information should be posted in a central location. Many employees would like to better themselves and without any incentives, job dissatisfaction is created.

(d) The Personnel Department should develop an attitude of helpfullness and to stand behind the employees for higher wages and benefits. A concensus of people I have discussed this with agree that the Personnel Department's attitude creates job dissatisfaction.

(e) Night activities be developed for employees who live on the hospital grounds. Films that are being shown to the patients during the day could be used at night for the employees. Many employees have no transportation to leave the hospital grounds thereby causing very little to do after completing their shift.

(f) Picnics and other day time activities should be developed during the summer months as opposed to having only the once a year Employee Appreciation Day.

(g) An employee newsletter that would be sent each month by mail to each employee in the hospital , describing new developments, listings of new employees, retirees, their accomplishments, information from departments that would be newsworthy, and general informational stories and events. It could also be available upon request from employees no longer working for the hospital who would like to stay informed. The newsletter could be formulated by the Public Relations Department and would be separate from the patient newspaper, the Grapevine. This publication could be read by the employees' family and would be instrumental in showing the family where the employee works and how he is a part of this hospital. It could also show the employee that he is important and needed. This is important not only in strengthening family relationships, but letting the hospital communicate with the family.

10. The hospital should take full control of the Rehab Store, employing its own staff, maintenance, policing the grounds, and lowering prices with the profits returning to the hospital for patient activities. I would also suggest that the store remain open 7 days a week instead of 6.

Over twenty years ago the hospital ran the store but ran into problems when a "trusted employee embezelled" money. Since then, the Vocational Rehabilatation for the Blind Agency has taken charge. The hospital pays upkeep, water and power, supposedly general maintenance and in return we receive approximately 3% of their profits. We also get in return higher prices for the patients, unsanitary conditions, no supervision of patient activities, and fire and health hazards.

In 1973 the Medical Staff called for an audit of the store's prices to see if their prices were competitive with other stores that size. I assisted in that audit and we found the prices much higher than local stores. This was reported back to the Medical Staff and no further action was taken. It should also be noted that some members of the Medical Staff instruct their patients to go in groups to the store because of the dangerousness due to the fact that there is no supervision of patient activities. There have been numerous reports from patients that they are able to buy drugs and alcohol at the store and that it is done openly.

It is my understanding that a survey team from the Social Security Administration found the store deplorable and a summary of their findings will be sent to the Administration in the very near future. If there is just cause, the Mississippi Medicaid Commission can survey the Store to see if the prices are "reasonable", since there will probably be Medicaid payments made to this hospital in the future for all qualified residents.

In February of 1976 the Harrison County Association for Mental Health toured the hospital and "were further impressed by the cleanliness of the areas". "The one exception to this is the Canteen".

Mr. M.W. Burnham, Fire Chief, inspected the Rehab Store on 12/5/77 and a copy of that report is attached.

The Patient's Finance Committee, of which I am a member, submitted a proposal on 12/12/77 which is attached. In the guidelines for operating the present store until the hospital could operate it, only 2 are being maintained; D and E. If the hospital does not take control of the Store, it is quite possible the State Board of Health and the State Fire Codes could close it down. All of these problem could be alleviated if something other than talk was possible. It is obvious that the Store will continue to be a sore thumb of this hospital as it is, unless there is strong support from the Hospital Staff members to back up the Finance Committee's proposals.

11. I suggest that the Hospital Information Management Team oversee the six sub-committees they developed on 2/16/78 to see that these committees meet and carry out their duties and responsibilities. If there was enough thought in developing the committees, I would think there would be some device to see that they were implemented.

cc: Mr. Doyce B. Ward
Mr. Jim Nettles
Mr. James C. Stubbs

Memo to Sidney Tatum. Personal Copy

I continued to switch the outside lights off until my last day working at Whitfield.

Fred Chaney, "The King of Whitfield"

Fred Chaney, a long-time patient at Whitfield, was well known for smuggling letters out of the hospital during the 1940s and 1950s. In his letters, he described the conditions of the hospital, the food, politics, administration, his proposals, and recommendations for improvements. When he was caught sending these uncensored letters out of the hospital, he would be locked up in the Building for Disturbed Patients. He was, however, successful with his letters reaching Hodding Carter Jr., Owner and Editor of the *Delta Democrat-Times* in Greenville, Mississippi. Carter printed Fred's description of the conditions at Whitfield and his recommendations to correct those problems. At least I was not sent to the Disturbed Building, as Fred Chaney was for writing recommendations to the administration. The Disturbed Building was a locked building at the hospital that housed criminals, dangerous patients, noncompliance with the rules, punishments, patients who were at risk of escaping, and patients who were punished. The building was later condemned.

Fred was a patient in one of the cottages assigned to me. He was bedridden during the brief time that I was his social worker. When I asked him if he needed anything, he said he only wanted me to bring him a cigar to chew on. The charge nurse on the building told me he was called "The King of Whitfield," and if I wanted to know more about his life at Whitfield, I should research his letters and documents at the Mississippi Department of Archives and History. I read with amazement the story written by him over fifty years ago while he was a patient at Whitfield, who asked that his story be told.

Fred Clark Chaney was the great-grandson of Civil War Governor Charles Clark, a cousin to Walter Sillers Jr. and a friend of *Delta Democrat-Times* editor Hodding Carter Jr. Fred was a man of vision, a lawyer, a prolific writer, and crusader who wanted the story of his mental illness and his mental hospitalization told to anyone who would listen. And often they did.

Fred spent the greater part of his adult life confined: first at St. Elizabeth's Hospital in Washington, DC in 1926, a few years later in Mississippi State Insane Asylum in 1932, and lastly at the Mississippi State Hospital at Whitfield, Mississippi, in 1939. He had numerous admissions, escapes, paroles, and discharges, making Whitfield his home until his death in 1975.

In the early days of his institutionalization, communications about the care and treatment of patients were censored by hospital staff. However, he smuggled his observations about the hospital in letters to his mother in Greenville, Mississippi, who would send them to Hodding Carter Jr. Carter took great interest in Chaney's insightful letters about the conditions at Whitfield and published his correspondence which was shared with newspapers across the state. His editorials about Chaney and Whitfield brought about numerous investigations by the Mississippi Legislature, the Mississippi Medical Association, the governor's office, the Legislative Audit Committee, and the Mississippi Department of Mental Health. Dr. William Jaquith, former director of Whitfield, often said that it was Fred Chaney who was instrumental, through his letters, in alerting the public about the deteriorating conditions at Whitfield.

Mr. Chaney had many connections with politicians, community leaders, and newspaper editors who engaged in his institutionalization as well as other causes he championed. He submitted lengthy epistles and letters about his patients' work-for-pay proposals, the issue surrounding maximum security for the criminally insane, the admission laws to Whitfield, vocational rehabilitation, civil rights, and harnessing Mississippi's waterways for power supply and transportation. He was known for writing letters that would sometimes number 90 pages or more.

Fred Chaney's story touches on many distinct aspects of twentieth-century Mississippi culture. Chaney's exploits and escapes from both the Mississippi State Insane Hospital and the Mississippi State Hospital provide an inside look at the dehumanizing effects of earlier treatments of the mentally ill.

Mississippi's history prior to and after the Civil War and Chaney's involvement in politics are vividly described and detailed in Mr. Chaney's letters and manuscripts as well as through family accounts and interviews. His eyewitness account of the 1927 Mississippi River Flood and his manuscript titled "A Refugee's Story" will be of great interest to historians of the South. Advocates of the care of the mentally ill will appreciate Mr. Chaney's social commentary on the incarceration of the criminally insane, the establishment of work-for-pay programs for patients, vocational rehabilitation, and patient workers. His beliefs on segregation, as well as his lobbying key members of the legislature and the governor's office for more staff, funding, and resources for the Mississippi State Hospital, are also noteworthy.

It was Chaney's perseverance that drew me in as to how he wanted to make Whitfield a better place for the patients, staff, and administration. I suppose it was his willingness to take on that role that inspired me to write about my observations and recommendations while working at Mississippi State Hospital.

I have written a biography of Fred Chaney which I hope will be published in the future. However, more information about his life can be found at the Mississippi Department of Archives and History, and through my website at www.kingofwhitfield.com.

MISSISSIPPI STATE HOSPITAL

W. L. Jaquith, M.D.
Chief of Medical Staff

WHITFIELD, MISS.

James C. Stubbs
Director

July 17, 1978

Mr. Doyce B. Ward, Director
Social Work Department
Mississippi State Hospital
Whitfield, Mississippi

Dear Mr. Ward:

This is to inform you that as of this date I regretfully submit my resignation of employment with The Mississippi State Hospital. I have accepted another position with State Government which places me in a higher pay grade with a substantial salary increase. My last day of employment will be August 31, 1978.

As you know, I have always had a close attachment for Whitfield. Until recently, I have found much satisfaction in my job and have found working with patients rewarding; however, these things are not sufficient when there are no financial incentives or prospects for advancement in the future. I am also concerned that Administration does not reflect very much interest in the morale of hospital employees, particularly those who have had long standing service with the hospital. I feel that administration has overlooked our department in many respects, the details of which I am sure you are already familiar.

I appreciate the efforts you have made to improve things in our department. If the above situations are resolved, I would welcome the opportunity to return to the hospital to work if the opportunity arises.

Sincerely,

Ernest Bowen

Ernest Bowen
Social Worker

cc: Mr. James Stubbs
Dr. Glenn Anderson
Mr. Ken Millis

Memo to Mr. Ward. Resignation Letter. Personal Copy

Employee of the Month - Really?

Each month the hospital honors two employees as Employees of the Month. Fellow employees suggest someone and complete a form providing the reason that person should be recognized. There is an Employee of the Month Selection Committee who reviews the forms and makes the decision. I was selected as the Employee of the Month for August 1978 after I submitted my resignation. I found it interesting that I was chosen but realized, too, that honor is more about work than office antics.

That photo was in the August 10, 1978, issue of *The Grapevine.* For the record I had long hair and a moustache. The following documents from my personnel file were provided to me when I retired:

Below are pages from *The Grapevine* recognizing all the Employees of the Month and copies of documents from the personnel department.[21]

Mississippi State Hospital

MISSISSIPPI STATE HOSPITAL
BETTER MENTAL HOSPITALS
BETTER MENTAL HEALTH

CERTIFICATE OF APPRECIATION TO

ERNEST L. BOWEN

as Employee of the Month for AUGUST, 1978
for dedicated and outstanding service to
Mississippi State Hospital.

AUGUST 1, 1978
DATE

DIRECTOR

EMPLOYEES OF THE MONTH - AUGUST, 1978

Above (Left to Right):
James C. Stubbs, Hospital Director
Doyce Ward, Director of Social Service
E. "Bunny" Bowen, Employee of the Month - August
Mrs. Mae Roberts, Director of Nursing Service, Female Services
Paul Jent, Chairman, Employee of the Month Selection Committee
Mrs. Nazaree Callaway, Employee of the Month - August

—MRS. SHERRI GRIMES
ADMINISTRATIVE ASSISTANT

[See Special Feature on Pages 2 - 3]

)* * *(

MISSISSIPPI STATE HOSPITAL

W. L. Jaquith, M.D.
Chief of Medical Staff

WHITFIELD, MISS.

James C. Stubbs
Director

TO: Mrs. Christine McNeel, Dietitian

FROM: James C. Stubbs, Director J.C.S.

SUBJECT: Employee of the Month Meal Ticket

Mr. Ernest Bowen has been selected as Employee of the Month for August, 1978. As an additional recognition I am authorizing a meal ticket at no cost to him.

I have for your convenience provided 15 numbers at the bottom of this Memo that are to be handled as is any other meal ticket.

1 / 2 / 3 / 4 / 5 / 6 / 7 / 8 / 9 / 10

11 / 12 / 13 / 14 / 15.

Employee Signature

EMPLOYEES OF THE MONTH - AUGUST

In the year of 27 B.C. until 14 A.D. a life style of elegance was enjoyed by a man by the name of Augustus Caesar. This man was powerful. More to the point, he was dictatorial. As one of his fancies, he decided to change the calendar and add a month named in his honor.

Today the eighth month of our calendar is named after this figure in history—August.

As did Caesar want to honor himself, so do we wish to take this month to honor two outstanding employees as Employees of the Month. Both of these employees are highly admired and respected by their fellow employees, and both received numerous recommendations.

ERNEST "BUNNY" BOWEN, Social Worker, joined the Staff of Mississippi State Hospital six and one-half years ago.

DR. CHARLES MANGIN states: "I am recommending MR. BOWEN on the basis of my impressions concerning his abilities after having worked together with him on numerous and oftentimes difficult patient problems. His comprehension, concern, and resolution of these problems have been exceptionally professional and effective. His personal rapport with the patients and his fellow workers has been of a quality that has produced good results and harmonious interpersonal relationships. It is actually a pleasure for me to make such a recommendation."

MS. HATTIE SPEARS, Reimbursement Department Supervisor, writes: "MR. BOWEN works diligently and openly in responding to the needs of both the patients and the hospital administration. He has demonstrated initiative, reliability, and industriousness while working with this department. He has been remarkably tactful and cooperative in dealing with the families and concerned parties of his patients. These attributes, complemented by his social work ability and experience, deserve our praise."

PAUL JENT, Social Services Supervisor, comments: "He has been one of the most conscientious employees with whom I have worked. I have seen him work diligently to provide services for his patients in spite of many obstacles and have known him to change his personal plans for vacations or days off in order to complete necessary paperwork to get patients into a nursing home while beds were available.

"MR. BOWEN has carried one of the largest case loads of any worker on the Social Work Staff, and, in spite of the pressures he has faced in maintaining an increasing caseload and additional responsibilities, he has

(Continued on next page)

EMPLOYEES OF THE MONTH - AUGUST (CONTINUED)

managed to keep a good sense of humor and a very good rapport with those around whom he works. He has certainly put his best into his work and is worthy of recognition."

As this article was being written it was discovered that MR. BOWEN will be leaving the Hospital on September 1. He has accepted a position that will be enabling him to further advance his professional capabilities. Our loss will be their gain!

MRS. NAZAREE CALLAWAY, LPN on Building 23, has been a dedicated MSH employee for 25 years.

MS. ETHEL M. SMITH, MS. DELLA MAE BROWN, and MS. CHARLOTTE MOORE state: "MRS. CALLAWAY is a very experienced and dedicated employee. She is always willing and ready to help in any kind of situation concerning her fellow workers and especially in the care of patients. Her 25 years at MSH are highly recognized by all who know her."

MS. BARBARA WOMACK comments: "MRS. CALLAWAY is an outstanding person to work with. She also helps to make the patients to feel wanted and cared for.

"Her pleasing personality and understanding have helped many patients and also employees get over some of their problems. She always has a listening ear. She always helps with the work load."

Other fellow workers state: "She is a good supervisor and one that knows her job and tries to cooperate with her fellow employees. She instructs employees on how to do their best in caring for the patients. We all feel that she has made an outstanding contribution to Mississippi State Hospital."

"August is a good month," states JAMES C. STUBBS, Director of the Hospital, "and it is also a good time to honor two such well-deserving employees as Employees of the Month." He continues, "I join with all employees in honoring these outstanding employees."

—MRS. SHERRI GRIMES
ADMINISTRATIVE ASSISTANT

[See Photo on Page 1]

EMPLOYEE OF THE MONTH NOMINATION

7/20/78
(Date)

NAME OF SUGGESTED EMPLOYEE Ernest Bowen

LENGTH OF SERVICE 6 1/2 Years

EMPLOYEE TITLE Social Worker A

PLACE OF EMPLOYMENT (Building) Administration

Complete the following sentence with as much information as to why you are suggesting this employee as Employee of the Month.

I am suggesting Ernest Bowen (Name of Employee) for Employee of the Month because:

He is a very fine young man to begin with. He is a very conscientious Social Worker and knows all his patients by name and takes care of their immediate needs. He is very prompt in getting to work and is courteous to every one. He carries the largest patient case load on the Social Work Staff. I have observed that he handles the largest paper work load on the staff. In spite of all pressure of his responsibility He has still maintained his great sense of humor. I think he very much deserves this award

**Use additional pages if needed.

Signed: Nellie Martin
(Employee(s) making nomination)

Department Head signature

AAAAAAAAAAAAAAAAAAAAAAA

Date application received

E M P L O Y E E   O F   T H E   M O N T H   N O M I N A T I O N

July 19, 1978
(Date)

NAME OF SUGGESTED EMPLOYEE Ernest L. Bowen

LENGTH OF SERVICE 6 years

EMPLOYEE TITLE Institutional Social Worker I

PLACE OF EMPLOYMENT(Building) ____________

Complete the following sentence with as much information as to why you are suggesting this employee as Employee of the Month.

I am suggesting Ernest Bowen (Name of Employee) for Employee of the Month because: He has been one of the most consciencious employees with whom I have worked. During his tenure at this hospital I have seen Mr. Bowen work diligently to provide services for his patients in spite of some pretty significant obstacles. I have known Mr. Bowen to change his personal plans to have days off in order to complete all the necessary paperwork to get patients into a nursing home while beds were available. I have observed Mr. Bowen using his personal vehicle to haul dozens of cartons of cokes he has purchased for Building 34. Mr. Bowen has carried one of the largest case loads of any worker on the social work staff and in spite of the pressures he has faced in maintaining an increasing caseload and additional responsibilities, he has managed to keep a good sense of humor and a very good raport with those around whom he works. Of all the social work staff, Mr. Bowen probably tops the list in the quality and volume of the paperwork he handles. Case records on his patient load reflect the volume and quality of his written work as well as good doccumentation of all the services he has provided for his patients. Over the years Mr. Bowen has developed detailed knowledge of the patients he has served which to me reflects a very caring attitude. While Mr. Bowen's length of service to this hospital may be less than others, he has certainly put his best into his work and is worthy of recognition.

**Use additional pages if needed.

Signed: Paul Jent
(Employee(s) making nomination)

____
Department Head signature
XXXXXXXXXXXXXXXXXXXXXXXXXX
Date application received
____

EMPLOYEE OF THE MONTH NOMINATION

7-19-78
(Date)

NAME OF SUGGESTED EMPLOYEE Ernest (Bunny) Bowen

LENGTH OF SERVICE 6 years

EMPLOYEE TITLE Institutional Social Worker I

PLACE OF EMPLOYMENT(Building) Administration Bldg.

Complete the following sentence with as much information as to why you are suggesting this employee as Employee of the Month.

I am suggesting Ernest Bowen (Name of Employee) for Employee of the Month because: He is a very conscientious worker who is certainly an advocate for his patients. He is through in his casework and picks up on points that many other workers have missed through the years that proves to be of help to his patients. He is willing to assist with duties in the office whether it falls under his job description or not. I have seen him go that "extra mile," that is required of social workers, many times since I have known him. He is interested in ongoing education in his field. He is a very likeable person to work with.

**Use additional pages if needed.

Signed: Mary Adkins
(Employee(s) making nomination)

Department Head signature
****
Date application received

EMPLOYEE OF THE MONTH NOMINATION

7-19-78
(Date)

NAME OF SUGGESTED EMPLOYEE Ernest C. Bowen III

LENGTH OF SERVICE about 6 years

EMPLOYEE TITLE Social Worker I

PLACE OF EMPLOYMENT (Building) Administration

Complete the following sentence with as much information as to why you are suggesting this employee as Employee of the Month.

I am suggesting "Bunny" Bowen for Employee of
(Name of Employee)
the Month because: he is and has been dedicated to quality patient care and this is reflected by his concern and work with his patients. He is always ready to try new methods of working with his patients and their rehabilitation. Mr. Bowen strives to lessen the patient's trauma of hospitalization and mitigate their length of stay. He is always ready to lend a "helping hand" to co workers, and he is quite knowlegeable of community resources and how they can benefit his patients as well as the hospital. He is most dedicated to his work!

**Use additional pages if needed.

Signed: Michael F Edwards
(Employee(s) making nomination)

Department Head signature
****
Date application received

E M P L O Y E E   O F   T H E   M O N T H   N O M I N A T I O N

7-19-78
(Date)

NAME OF SUGGESTED EMPLOYEE Earnest Bowen

LENGTH OF SERVICE

EMPLOYEE TITLE Social Worker

PLACE OF EMPLOYMENT (Building) Administration Bldg.

Complete the following sentence with as much information as to why you are suggesting this employee as Employee of the Month.

I am suggesting ______________ (Name of Employee) for Employee of the Month because: he is one of the nicest and courteous people I've ever had the pleasure to know. He is always interested in improving the hospital conditions. Whenever I need help in regard to one of his patients, he is always helpful and patient. Also Earnest is very consciencious and thorough in keeping our dept. informed on changes in patient status. It is my opinion that he has been a real asset to Mississippi State Hospital.

**Use additional pages if needed.

Signed: Marion E. Abt
(Employee(a) making nomination)

Department Head signature
Date application received

E M P L O Y E E   O F   T H E   M O N T H   N O M I N A T I O N

7/19/78
(Date)

NAME OF SUGGESTED EMPLOYEE Ernest Bowen

LENGTH OF SERVICE around 6 yrs.

EMPLOYEE TITLE Social Worker

PLACE OF EMPLOYMENT(Building) Social Services/Administration Bldg.

Complete the following sentence with as much information as to why you are suggesting this employee as Employee of the Month.

I am suggesting Ernest Bowen (Name of Employee) for Employee of the Month because: he has been a truely dedicated worker. He has gone above and beyond his regular duties in the interest of the patients he works with. Bowen has a wonderful sense of humor which is an asset to the morale of the Social Service Department. We will all be sorry to see him leave but are happy that his new job will allow him to reach his full potential.

**Use additional pages if needed.

Signed: Susan Lundquist
(Employee(s) making nomination)

Department Head signature
AAAAAAAAAAAAAAAAAAAAAAAAA
Date application received

EMPLOYEE OF THE MONTH NOMINATION

2/28/78
(Date)

NAME OF SUGGESTED EMPLOYEE Ernest L. Bowen

LENGTH OF SERVICE Too Long

EMPLOYEE TITLE Sociable Worker

PLACE OF EMPLOYMENT(Building) Administration

Complete the following sentence with as much information as to why you are suggesting this employee as Employee of the Month.

I am suggesting Ernest Bowen (Name of Employee) for Employee of the Month because: He needs a fifteen day meal ticket and an extra day off. You see – Ernest bought a new pick-up truck and ever since he bought it he has had diarrhea wondering how he was going to pay for it. He needs the day off so he can stop the "trots". Secondly, Mr. Bowen needs the fifteen day meal ticket so he can "refuel". This will ~~also~~ also relieve his incessant worry that he will not be able to eat because he bought his new truck

**Use additional pages if needed.

Signed: Mortimer Snerd
(Employee(s) making nomination)

Department Head signature
AAAAAAAAAAAAAAAAAAAAAAAAAA
Date application received

And then there had to be a funny nomination. This one is from Paul Jent.

OUR "EMPLOYEE OF THE MONTH"

He walks the halls in faded jeans,
His Floppy hair is long - it seems.
His ragged beard --- It seems to fit,
Looks like it came from his arm pit.
He pulls a cig and lights it up,
And walks around with coffee cup.
He wanders around from desk to desk -
To figure how to be a pest;
He teases Hattie, Liz and Judy...
It is his bound and faithful duty
To see how devilish he can be;
He'll drive you to insanity!
In case this fellow you're not knowin,
Tis the one and only Bunny Bowen.

Paul Jent was a social worker and good friend who had enormous talent in writing poems, limericks, and fake memos. His sense of humor and playful tricks, especially on me, were outstanding. Many times, it seemed as if we were competing to see who could write the funniest memo to staff who were under the watchful eye of Doyce Ward, the Social Work Director. Mr. Ward called me out on many animated conversations and acts around the office. I have evaluations from him that said I needed to pay more attention to my work rather than my office activities. This was well before I was assigned larger caseloads and responsibilities. But reading the nomination forms will show that I must have done a decent job.

Mr. Jent and I often added special reports for *The Grapevine*. Of course, our reports were typed into an existing issue and shared only with some staff who understood the humor. In the March 9, 1978, *Grapevine*, Paul wrote the following:

Social Service Report

It is reported in Social Service that Mr. Ernest Bowen has reached the "ripe" age of thirty. By his behavior, we would say that Mr. Bowen is not only "ripe" but rotten! Hats off to Mr. Bowen for being selected "Crab of The Month."

New Royal Hotel, "In the Heart of the Business District"

Several months after I started work in Social Services, I received a letter from Booker T. Sot, assistant manager with the New Royal Hotel dated June 14, 1972. I am certain it was a Paul Jent stunt. This letter was to confirm my reservation for the honeymoon suite for the weekend of June 23-25th. And he hoped that my new wife and I would be happy with the accommodation.

Pranks and Laughs

I considered myself one of the pranksters at Whitfield. I played tricks on social service staff – some that were not that funny. But I was not the only one. There were several other social workers who got into writing funny memos to staff, bizarre phone messages and even going as far as completing patient assessment forms on staff. I was caught more times than the other staff, usually by Doyce Ward. I pressed my luck with him by continuing to make light of some of the hospital and social service rules. At Whitfield it helped to have a sense of humor.

Personnel Policies?

All employees are given a copy of the Hospital Employees' Personnel Policies. After reading the policies, I decided that there were a few rules that I felt were unfair to the employee, and, if anything, would promote poor morale. I discovered the typewriter font the personnel office used for their memos and used our office typewriter to make a replica of the form and replaced "will" to "not" abide to those rules. I sent the form to the personnel office. No one was the wiser. Until now.

ACKNOWLEDGEMENT OF PERSONNEL POLICIES

I have read and understand the personnel policies outlined in the handbook on the various rules, regulations, and benefits which apply to me as an employee of this institution. In consideration of my employment by this institution and knowing that my employment is not dependent upon my compliance to these rules and regulations, I will not follow these guidelines at all times.

DATE:________________ Signature:____________________

SIGNED

The Meal Ticket

The special Christmas meal ticket was given to all employees from the hospital to be used on only one specified day. Those who had to work the holidays would be given two days off at a later date. The last paragraph was added to Mr. Stubb's memo that I had placed on a bulletin board. It was noticed only by those staff whom I told. Other than that, it was just another hospital memo to staff.

MISSISSIPPI STATE HOSPITAL
PERSONNEL OFFICE
WHITFIELD, MISS.

December 21, 1977

TO: ALL EMPLOYEES

Friday, December 23 rd and Monday, December 26th will be holidays in observance of Christmas. A minimum staff of employees as scheduled by the Department Heads, will be required to work on these days to provide adequate patient care. Those employees working either Friday or Monday, December 23rd or 26th will be given two holidays at a later date for each of these days worked.

Monday, January 2, 1978 will be a holiday in observance of New Year's Day. Those employees scheduled to work on this day will be given one holiday at a later date as scheduled by their supervisor.

Ken Millis
Ken Millis
Personnel Director

TO: ALL EMPLOYEES

FROM: JAMES C. STUBBS, DIRECTOR

SUBJECT: SPECIAL CHRISTMAS MEAL--December 22, 1977.

All employees are required to present their meal tickets and/or their official identification card at the dining hall on December 22 for the Special Christmas Meal. In addition, all employees must wear their name badge.

Again, I would like to express my sincere wish that each of you have a Merry Christmas and a prosperous New Year.

*

In addition, all first born male children of those employees working the 8 to 4 shift will be required to show in writing and to be delivered to the Personnel Office, no later than Tuesday, December 29, 1977, a statement describing their parents thoughts and happiness during the two holidays that have been given to them by the Governor's Office.

It should be noted that if the statement does not reflect happiness during this holiday season, the first born male child will be required to work every other weekend at the Governor's Mansion picking up debris.

This was given to me by another social worker whose name I cannot remember.

DEPARTMENTAL CORRESPONDENCE

DATE 9/27/77

SUBJECT History

TO Mr. ERK Bowen DEPARTMENT housewares

FROM ? DEPARTMENT Lingerie

Hi

[Y] → [o]
↓
[U] → [A] → [r] → [e] → [S]
↓
[o]
↓
[S]
↓
[t]upid
↓
Go to 7734

(turn upside down)

do not pass go
do not collect 200°°d

A Treatment Plan for Social Workers

Social Workers had to complete the Social Work Treatment Plan on all their patients. Paul Jent completed my personal Treatment Plan.

PATIENT'S NAME Ernest Bowen

ADMISSION DATE: 5/1/75

HOSPITAL NUMBER: 000-000

SOCIAL WORK TREATMENT PLAN
Mississippi State Hospital

I. OBTAIN INFORMATION FROM FAMILY (Please check method used and record date)

- A. Personal Interview: ✓ 5/1/75
- B. Telephone Interview: 5/1/75
- C. Letter from Family: 5/1/75
- D. Welfare Department Contact: 5/1/75
- E. Other: ________

II. ORIENTATION OF FAMILIES TO HOSPITAL PROCEDURES AND SERVICES (Check appropiate one)

- A. Personal Interview and MSH Pamphlet ✓
- B. By Mail with letter and MSH Pamphlet ✓
- C. Telephone Contact: ✓
- D. Other: ________

III. INITIAL PATIENT INTERVIEW: (Date Conducted) 5/1/75

IV. ORIENTATION OF NEW PATIENTS TO WARD (Please Circle method(s) used)

- (A.) Individual session with patient
- (B.) Group Sessions
- (C.) Other, Please Specify: ________

V. ROUTINE ROUNDS AND CONFERENCE WITH DOCTORS (Comments, if indicated, to be recorded on patient's ward folder.)

VI. EXPLORATION OF FAMILY RELATIONSHIP:

- A. With Patient: ✓
- B. With Family: ✓
- C. Other, Please Specify: ✓ With probation officer

VII. IDENTIFICATION OF PATIENT'S NEEDS AND WORKER'S PLAN OF ACTION:

This pt's needs are multi-fold and are a real challenge to any S.W. Pt needs new clothes, a hair-cut, a salary increase, a T.V. in his office so he can watch "As the Stomach Turns" and a 5 year subscription to "Oui" magazine. He needs a lock on his office door to keep wandering social workers from messing with (or on) his desk. He also needs to mail the packages on his office floor and to remove the 1974 Cocola calendar from the closet door

PAGE 2; SOCIAL WORK TREATMENT PLAN ON: Bowen

D. SPECIAL SERVICES INDICATED (Please check Appropiate Line)

1. Boarding Home Placement:
2. Nursing Home Placement:
3. Deportation to Another Hospital: ✓ WITH SALARY INCREASE
4. Physician referral for eye exam, glasses, prothesis (Circle Appropiate Ones)
5. Teeth:
6. Walkers, Wheel Chairs:
7. Family Counseling:
8. Referral to Vo-Rehab.
9. Obtain Surgical and EST Permits: ✓ - FOR pre-FRONTAL LOBOTOMY UNder lOCAL TOPICAL ANESTHESIA
10. Other, Please Specify:
11. Other:
12. Other:
13. Other:
14. Other:
15. Other:

VIII. DISCHARGE PLANNING:

A. Assessment of Home Situation: POOR

B. Evaluation of Community Resources: EXhausTed

C. Referral To Aftercare Program: Needs before AND AFTER CARE

IX. IF PATIENT IS TRANSFERRED, PROVIDE CONTINUITY BETWEEN SERVICES:

Patient Transferred to: Date:

Brief Status Report: PATIENT has NO "STATUS"

5/1/75
Date:

I. P. Freely
Social Worker

MISSISSIPPI STATE HOSPITAL

W. L. Jaquith, M.D.
Chief of Medical Staff

WHITFIELD, MISS.

James C. Stubbs
Director

January 1, 1977

TO. All Employess at Mississippi State Hospital

FROM: Business Office, Payroll Dept.

RE: Identification Requirements for Payroll Checks

Beginning with your Janurary check complete Identification will be required for ALL checks. Identification will consist of

1. Identification Card
2. Name Tag

Both named above requirements were issued at the beginning of your employment with Mississippi State Hospital. Both must be presented at the Payroll window when picking up your check.

Another person will be allowed to pick up your check should you become ill or an extreme emergency arise. In order for another person to pick up your check the three following requirements must be met.

1. Identification Card
2. Name Tag
3. A signed note by the absent person stating his or her reason for absence.

This will apply only in the case of illness or extreme emergencies. No exceptions will be made by this office.

If identification is lost, a duplicate Name Tag can be obtained at the Personnel Office for a $1.00. A duplicated name card can be issued at the Payroll Office for a $1.00.

Absolutely all checks will be issued through the Payroll Office.

Sidney H. Tatum
Business Manager

What's my name again?

A new hospital rule for all employees required everyone to produce two forms of identification to receive their paycheck. I believe the only way to have access to our paycheck was with the actual check. There were no direct deposits at that time.

I again pushed my luck and went to the payroll window and asked for my check. My only identification was the name badge that all employees had to wear. Even though I knew everyone in the business office, I still had to produce two forms of identification.

I went back to my office and made a sign that I pinned on my shirt with all my identifying information, plus my driver's license and library card. Mr. Sidney Tatum, Director of the Business Office, gave me my check, but he was not amused.

The Santa "Clause" Wish List

No one was ever safe from a funny letter to "Santa Clause." Paul Jent wrote this letter, making it appear that it was coming from a lady in our secretarial pool.

Mr. Santa Clause
North Pole
The Universe, 00000

Re: My Christmas list

Dear Santa:

It has been a long time (60 plus years) since I have written you and asked for anything but I thought that before I go to the great beyond, that I would ask for several more things. Please bring me the following items:

First of all, I would like a printing press and some engraved plates to make one hundred dollar bills. Please don't forget to bring the right kind of paper so I wouldn't get in trouble with the U.S. Treasury Department for counterfeiting.

Secondly, I would like to have a new blower wheel for my trailer's forced air heating unit. My head sure gets hot and I get out of breath as I presently have to stick my head in the furnace and huff and puff to get the air moving in the ducts.

Thirdly, I would like for you to make me a jumbo size but compact folding, tear proof doggie bag that would be suitable for me to wear under my dress. Please make the opening at the pocket level so I can just ease things in my pocket through a hole into the doggie bag. It would also be nice to have a clear plastic pair of tongs that I could inconspiciously move across the table to reach goodies that are hard to reach.

Fourthly, I would like to have a 1912 Edison Electric Typewriter, you know, the one that has a generator you have to crank by hand to make the electricity. I prefer the model with the handle that you pull to make the carriage return.

Last, but not least, I would like a nice elderly gentleman, such as yourself but one with a lot of money and one foot in the grave and the other on a grease slick. I'm too old for any hanky panky so you better throw in an extra bed to boot. Please make sure that the man you bring washes his feet, doesn't belch in public and doesn't have bad breath (even though when it comes to me, I say that bad breath is better than no breath at all.)

Santa, I appreciate all the firewood you have brought me over the past sixty years. In this time of energy crisis, it sure has come in handy.

Love and kisses,

"Liz"

The Little Boy's Room

What started out as a request to fix the urinal in the Social Service's men's bathroom ended up being a source of humor from some of the male social workers. I was serious about the flies circling inside the urinal because the water had been turned off to one urinal. I pushed the envelope on this venture as well. And we all thought it was fun to discuss.

L. Jaquith, M.D.
of Medical Staff

WHITFIELD, MISS.

James C. St
Directo

April 27, 1976

MEMO

TO: Mr. Doyce Ward, Director
Social Work Department

FROM: Ernest Bowen, Social Worker EB

Re: Men's Restroom-Social Work Department

Over the last several weeks I have noticed some type of small flying insect around and in the urinal. To me this presents a health hazard to the male employees, visitors and patients. I suggest we have a plumber correct the flushing mechanism so there will be no standing water and would also suggest that the supervisor of housekeeping be notifiedofo the restroom conditions.

EB:el

The Urinal Analysis

Mr. Jent provided additional assistance in addressing the men's room with the following memo. It was certainly not distributed to all the staff. Paul Jent was "Chee Whiz" and took great pleasure in writing these memos about the urinal. We both thought it was funny, but at the same time, we wanted the urinal to work correctly. I needed to make a urinal analysis.

Paul Jent died several years ago, so his antics cannot be confirmed or protected.

MISSISSIPPI STATE HOSPITAL

W. L. Jaquith, M.D.
Chief of Medical Staff

WHITFIELD, MISS.

James C. Stubbs
Director

April 30, 1976

MEMO:

TO: Mr. E. Bowen, Social Worker

FROM: Housekeeping Department

RE: Flies in the bathroom

Please refer to previous memo requesting that you refrain from using the men's room on the second floor of the Administration Building. Now we realize that there is a need for you "to go" when you've got "to go." Because of this, we feel that we've come upon a solution and are giving you the enclosed which you can use in the privacy of your own office. This way there will be no more flies coming in for a landing and every-one will be happy.

Chee Whiz

Chee Whiz, Director
Housekeeping Department

Mr. Doyce Ward

Mr. Ward was a supervisor under Kathryn Guice, Social Services Director. When I first started work in the department, he was a slightly rotund man who kept his pants up high on his hips. Commonly called "High Pockets," he wore short-sleeve shirts, and his arms looked quite muscular. During the cold season, he wore a necklace of garlic cloves and often munched on fresh garlic. He said it kept people away from him and kept him from spreading germs. It worked. He became director after Ms. Guice's retirement.

I would often have lunch with Mr. Ward in the employees' dining hall. He would talk to me about my smoking habit, wishing that I would quit smoking because it was bad for my lungs. And I could not outrun him to the dining hall. I took him on. We started running on the sidewalk across from the general hospital, and, boy, he was fast. He was not built for speed, but could really turn on his running legs. I'm sure we were a sight to onlookers with us running at full gallop down the sidewalk. Yes, I was a bit breathless, but I beat him in the race.

While I was swarming around him like a stinging bee with all my crazy memos and office antics, we did get along. He often tried to find someone for me to date. But not social work staff.

Mr. Ward retired as Director of Social Services several years after I resigned in 1978. I attended his retirement party and got to see some old friends and reminisce about our times as social workers at Whitfield. Mr. Ward and I did not discuss any of my memos! He did, however, on my exit evaluation in August 1978, rate all my work as "very good." But he only rated me "good" in personal grooming. Could that have been based on my long hair and handlebar moustache? I respected Mr. Ward's wisdom and work ethic to the highest degree.

Patient Art, Poems, and Letters

Patients at Whitfield had opportunities to paint, draw, and write poems. Some of the artwork was very good, and I was honored by those patients in my service who wanted to give it to me. In addition to poems, my patients had written for me, I kept all the art they gave me. A few of the documents were lyrics to songs the patients had written. The hospital's Occupational Therapy Program gave the patients an outlet for their work. The Art Program taught them how to use assorted colors and to design what they were envisioning. Serendipity, the annual hospital art show, provided patients with an opportunity to exhibit and sell their work. All the art was framed, and many patients signed their names. There were no prices on the art, but they were sold instead through a silent auction. In addition to art, there were sculptures and ceramics. I have bought patient works of art at Serendipity that are now on my walls at home.

The patient art in this document was given to me over the years by patients in my different services. I blocked out their last names if they signed their art. Included are letters patients mailed to me and handed to me in their buildings.

I received a lot of letters from ladies in Female Receiving after they were discharged, and a few from patients in Receiving who wrote about their family problems and their addiction to alcohol and drugs. I also received letters from patients on the back service after they were discharged home or to a boarding home or nursing home in Jackson, Mississippi.

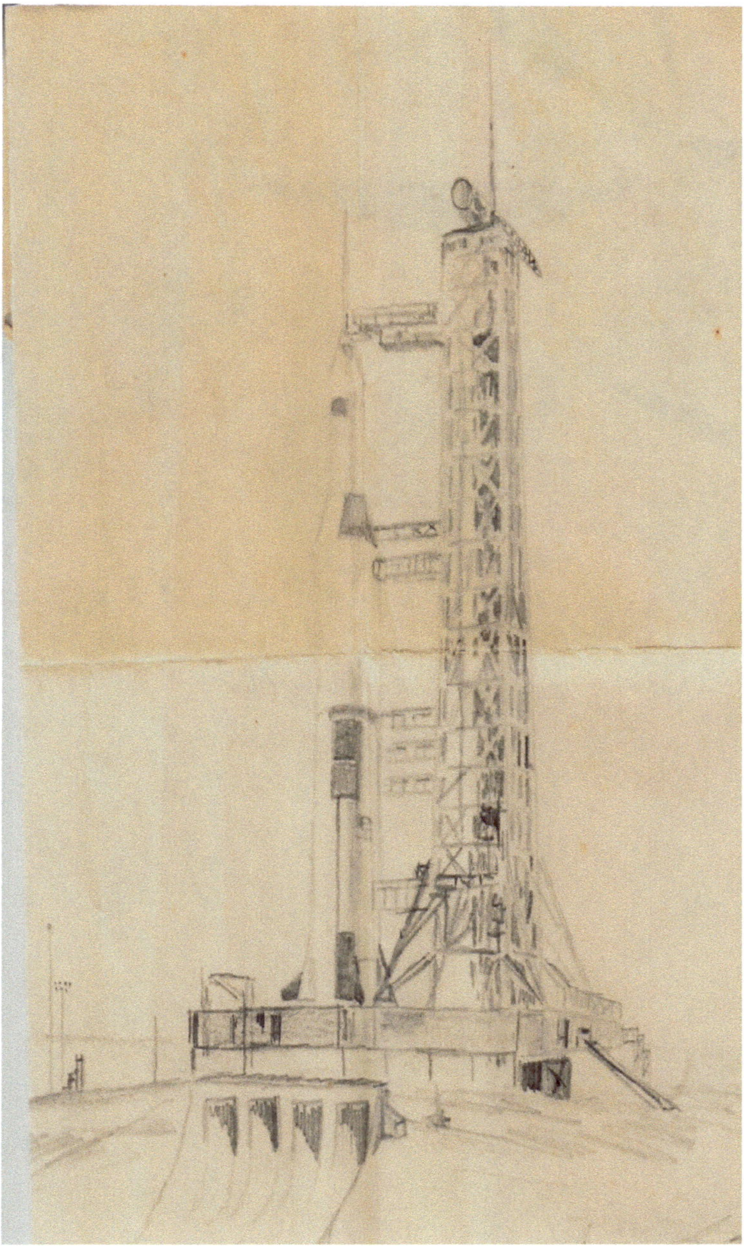

Charles Fortenberry signed and gave this art to me.

Mental Institution 21 Dec 72

Is a place where one
loses one's personality
To find the mistakes
that has pasted and Gone

One asks God to release
one of one's bondage
To find people who Run
the institution do not know
God. For I am god's child.

Now I've found myself
But will I be able To
exercise my Right
Of being a normal
Human Being again
Daddy Eugene come and
get me.
For I am not lost.
For God is my guide.

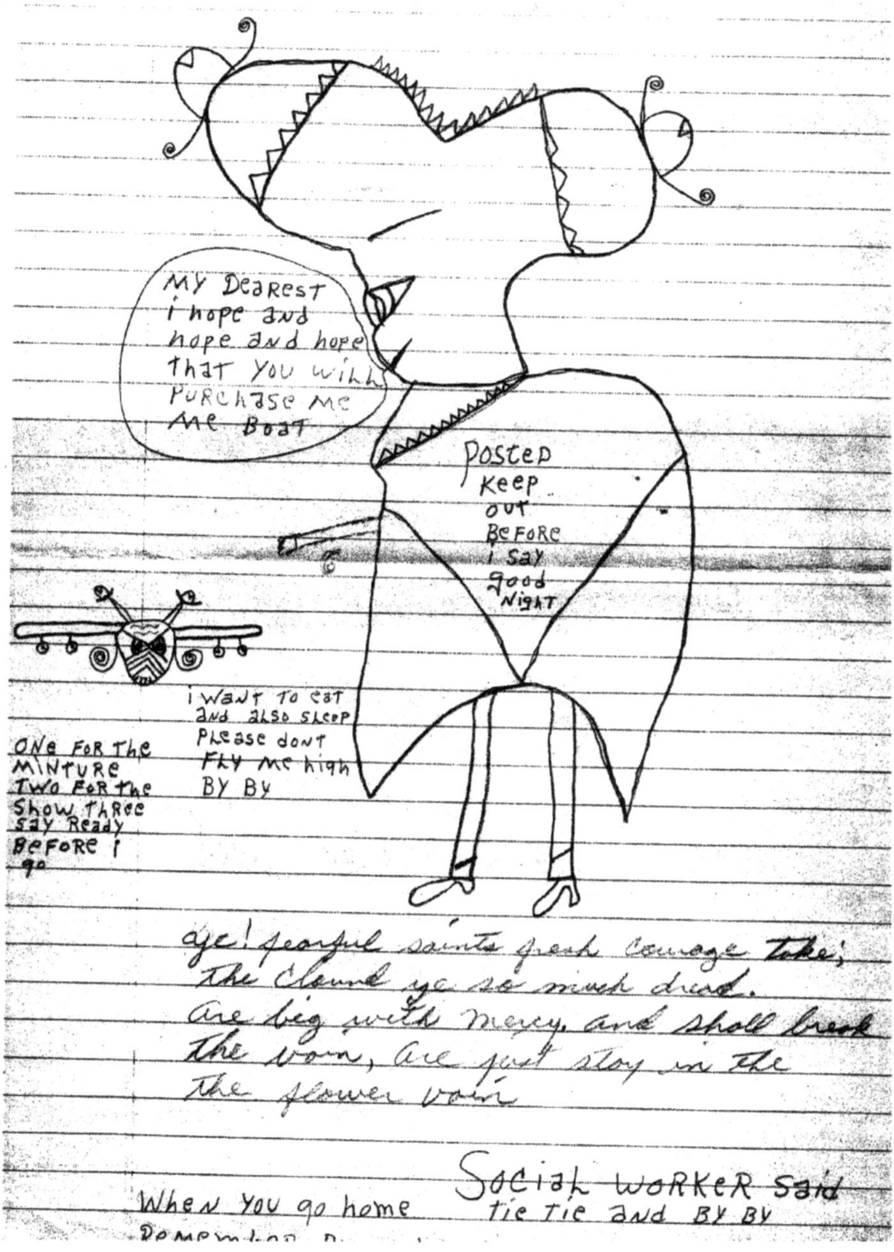

MY Dearest i hope and hope and hope that you will Purchase me Me Boat
Posted Keep out Before i say good Night
i want to eat and also sleep Please dont Fly me high BY BY
ONe FoR The MINTURE TWO FoR the Show THRee say Ready BeFORe I go
ye! fearful saints fresh courage take; the cloud ye so much dread. are big with mercy, and shall break the vain, are just stay in the the flower vain
Social worker said tie tie and BY BY
When you go home

MANIC

10/2/72

Dr. Brown the bird.
He doesn't give a
quack quack.

Clifton

MISSISSIPPI STATE HOSPI...
WHITFIELD, MISSISSIPPI 39193
The Times-Picayune
The Times-Picayune Publishing Corporation
3800 HOWARD AVENUE
NEW ORLEANS, LOUISIANA

MISSISSIPPI STATE HOSPITAL
PHYSICAL EXAMINATION AND
PROGRESS NOTES

Hospital No.

Service. Room No.

Name Larry Date April 4, 1970 Doctor

Praise Be to Nero's Neptune, the "Titanic's" sails at dawn, Everyone is shouting, which side are you on.

Sigmund Freud and Carl Jung fighting in the captain's towers, while calypso singers laugh at them and fisherman hold flowers.

Between the windows of the sea, where lovely mermaids flow and nobody has to think to much about Death Row.

Yes I received your letter yesterday, about the time the door knob broke when you ask me how I was feeling was that some kind of a joke?

All These people that you mentioned, yes I know they are quiet "lame." I had to rearrange their faces and gave them all another name.

Right now I can't read too good don't send me no more letters. No not unless you mail them from insanity Row.

Larry M. D.
SIGNATURE OF PHYSICIAN
April 4, 1970

To Bunny

Silently the wind blows over the fallen tree
Vague testimony to the mute silences of creation
Sighing, the wind passes in a trembling ecstasy
The ecstasy of eternal love

And the wind passes
And the wind sighs
And the wind moans
In its search for its partner – the sea.

And the sea calls
And the sea groans
And the sea is restless waiting for the wind

And the fallen tree is dead
And the fallen tree dies as it becomes
Part of the wind
And the fallen tree cries as it becomes
Part of the sea
The restless wind
And the restless sea
Of eternal thought
And eternity

WALTER
9/15/69

I must have told Walter to call me "Bunny"

I re-wrote this poem a patient let me read, and he asked that his original be placed in his medical record. We questioned if Larry was taking a line from a Bob Dylan song, "Desolation Row," when he changed it to "Insanity Row."

In the valley the Cattle are lowing,
Where the Skys are Pretty and Blue,
There are the dreams of the angles,
There live All the Horses we Need,
Old nelly - Old Billet, and Old Princes,
The ones that We All Understood
Under skys so blue And so Cloudy,
Like All the Prayers We knew,

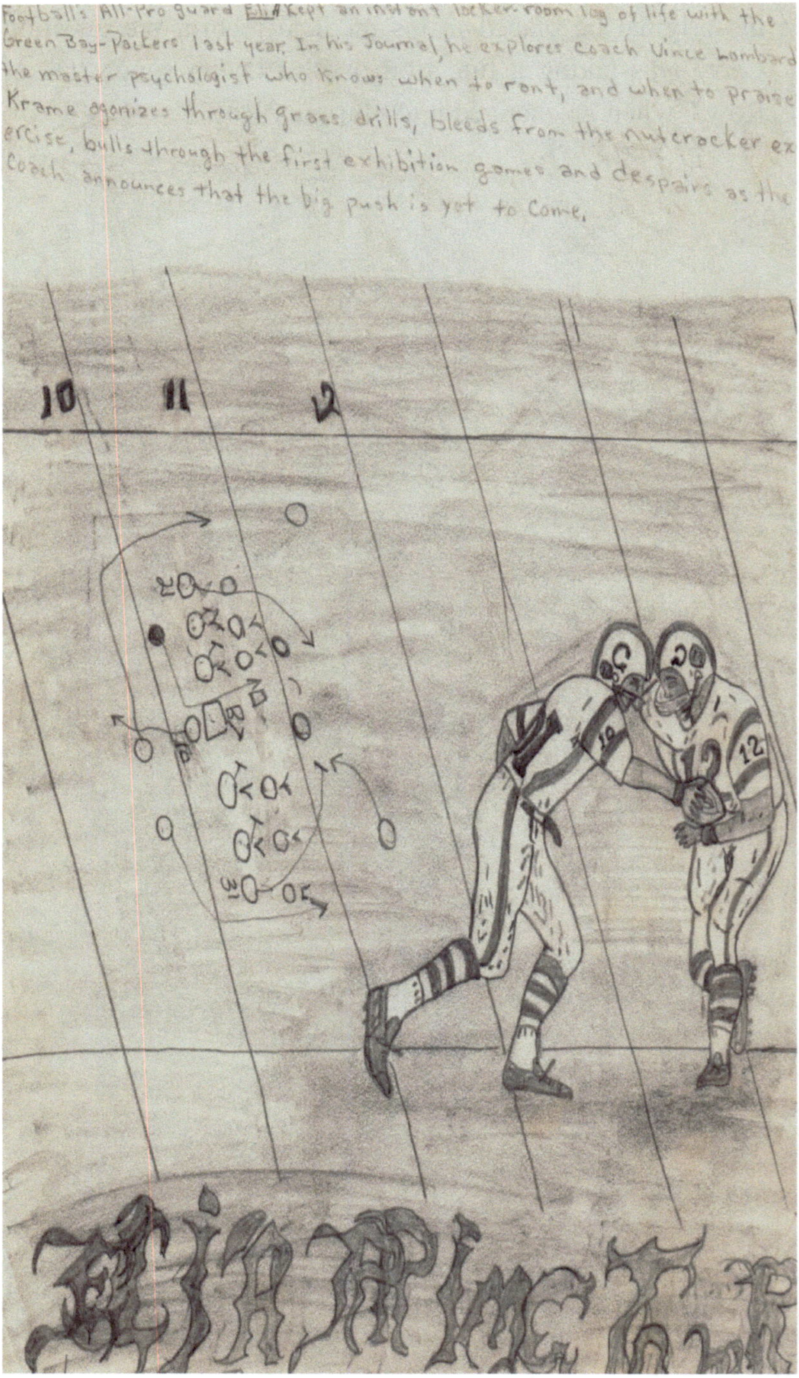
Football's All-Pro guard Eli Kept an instant locker-room log of life with the
Green Bay-Packers last year. In his Journal, he explores Coach Vince Lombard
the master psychologist who knows when to rant, and when to praise
Krame agonizes through grass drills, bleeds from the nutcracker ex
ercise, bulls through the first exhibition games and despairs as the
Coach announces that the big push is yet to Come.
10
11

Steve JAN - 1970

From the day you left my side
I've just sit right here and cried
a million tears that could never heal
The pain I've known loving you

Darlin I love you so
More than you will ever know
If only I had told you then
But now your gone.

Love is only and elusive dream
Something good but cruel sometimes
it seems

Someday way up ahead
We'll again walk hand & hand
and leave loves elusive dream
far behind

Pine Haven Road
Clinton Country manor, Nursing Home
Box 6 Clinton, Miss 37956
July 5, 1977

Dear Ernest Borden
Assistant Social
Waitfield, Miss.

Dear Ernest,

I was so glad of the help you gave us in bringing me over here April 26th.

We enjoy the meals here.

Ethel and Florence, two sisters, came to see me and showed me how to sew some on a slip.

I have played Bingo and embroidered some.

I appreciate your help very much. Can you come and get me. Dr. Fortenberry has gone for a vacation.

* And send me back to Cottage 48 or 36 or Hospital.

Lots of Love
Elizabeth

Letter to Ernest Bowen

August 4th,, 1977,

Ernest Dear;

Please come to the Library to see me this afternoon. I would like to know what day the four of us will leave here.

Love,

Louise St[illegible]n

MISSISSIPPI STATE HOSPITAL
WHITFIELD, MISSISSIPPI 39193

Mr. Ernest Boyd,
Social Worker,
c/o Administration Bldg
Whitfield, Miss.

NOTES

---

[1] Centennial Program, 1855-1955, Mississippi State Hospital, Whitfield, MS. Author's personal document.

[2] The Institutional Care of the Insane in the United States and Canada. 1916. Cornell University Library. http://www.archive.org/details. There are no known copyright restrictions in the United States on the use of the text.

[3] "Shellfire Threatened Old Institution During War, New Hospital for Insane Reaches its Finish," *Daily Clarion-Ledger,* Section Two, p.1, February 24, 1935.

[4] Allan Branstiter, "AHA Today, Madness and A Thousand Reconstruction: Learning to Embrace the messiness of the Past," The News Magazine of the American Historical Association. Summer, 2016.

[5] Mississippi State Hospital, Lucius M. Lampton, Mississippi Encyclopedia.

[6] James Gerald Paul, "Out of Darkness, Have I cried Unto thee: An examination of the treatment of African Americans at the Mississippi State Lunatic Asylum during Reconstruction (2017) https://egrove.olemiss.edu/hon_thesis/420

[7] "State's Insane Hospital Is Doing Laudable Work," *Daily Clarion-Ledger,* October 7, 1934.

[8] "New Plan Departure From Picturizations Of Typical Asylums," *Daily Clarion-Ledger,* Section Two, p. 2, February 24, 1935.

[9] The Mississippi State Hospital, Whitfield, Mississippi, October 1939, p.6. MDAH.

[10] "Believe it or Not!!!!! Isolated Remembrances (Hopefully Accurate) of the Early 70's to Early 80's at Mississippi State Hospital, Dr. William (Bill) Parker.

[11] Ibid.

[12] Psychiatry Online, September 10, 2020.

[13] Dr. Bill Parker, "Believe it or Not."

[14] Charles Gordon, Building 90, "Nine Days in a Nut House."

[15] Dr. Bill Parker, "Believe it or Not."

[16] Dr. William Jaquith Interview, April 10, 1979, MDAH.

[17] Ibid.

[18] Dr. Bill Parker, "Believe it or Not."

[19] Ibid.

[20] Charles Fortenberry obituary. *Clarion-Ledger*, December 1, 2014.

[21] Employee of the Month, *The Grapevine*, August 10,1978.

Made in United States
Troutdale, OR
11/03/2026

56844385R00090